enforcing

purpose

Lisa L. Schwarz

Enforcing Purpose
Copyright © 2020 Lisa L. Schwarz

ISBN: 978-1-7340693-1-0

Contact the author:
Lisa Schwarz
www.Lisa-Schwarz.com
www.Crazy8Ministries.com

Also by Lisa L. Schwarz:
Enforcing You
ISBN: 978-1-7340693-0-3

Mastering Your Seasons
ISBN: 978-0-692-75960-8

To Love and To Be Loved
ISBN: 978-1-978480-31-5

Discipleship: From Information to Execution
ISBN: 978-1-500192-59-4

Greek and Hebrew word translations taken from Blue Letter Bible. www.BlueLetterBible.org

Edited / Formatted by Kimberly Soesbee
www.KimberlySoesbee.com

Contents

Preface

Enforcing Purpose is written specifically as a sequel to my book *Enforcing You*. Although this book could stand-alone, enforcing purpose in your life can be very frustrating if it is pursued before you are confident and affluent in your God-design. *Enforcing You* provides practical teaching to help you take charge of who you are—your God-design—and manifest it in the way you act—your personality. "Enforcing you" means you view yourself from heaven's perspective and allow heaven's principles to become the reality of who you are. *Enforcing Purpose,* however, speaks of taking charge of what is in your heart (or in the heart of a mission) and bringing it to the surface. It is manifesting what you have always dreamt about and seeing it executed in the way you live your life. When working with people, I have found that before we can hone in on how to enforce their purpose, we have to enforce who they are!

I have had both of these messages burning in my heart for many years. They are near to my heart because they capture what I do daily as a counselor and as a life coach. As a counselor, I speak to the identity of an individual, his or her unique design. As a life coach, I speak to one's purpose—the dream of an individual. In counseling, we look at where we have been. In life coaching, we look to where we are going. One is looking back, while the other is looking forward. Both are necessary. Isn't it true that it can be frustrating trying to set sail when there are anchors in our lives? Conversely, isn't it true that once we remove our anchors, we also need to know how to find the winds and navigate them if we want to set sail? One without the other will keep us stuck or standing still in life. Either way, we are not moving forward and sailing toward our destiny. We must understand how they work in tandem to propel us into the fulfillment of our passions.

I have come to the full belief that the number one reason the enemy wants to keep you from enforcing who you are designed to be is so that you will never step into your purpose. It is possible to spend your whole life searching for your identity and purpose and then never do anything with it. A mentor of mine, Brian Holmes, wrote a book called *The Four Cornerstones for Strategic Living*. To sum it up, he teaches that the four cornerstones are personal healing, personal discovery, personal development, and personal deployment. In his work, he mentions that many people cycle through the first three cornerstones but never learn how to deploy. I think this is the enemy's biggest deception. He wants to steal, kill, and destroy your life, and part of the way he does this is by keeping you from your dreams and your purpose (see John 10:10). We can have life, as long as we don't do anything with it. In this manner, we are ineffective and ultimately will not have the impact that God intended for us. I am saying to you that it is possible to be alive but live as though you are dead—ineffective and without purpose. James 2:14-17 addresses this very thing; to have faith without any deployment is dead.

Much like *Enforcing You*, this book is designed to not just inspire you, but to empower you by equipping you with practical tools. In fact, I have included many of my coaching worksheets in this book. It is my desire to help you discover your purpose and activate it. There is nothing more frustrating than having a dream, a stirring in the heart, but never seeing it come to pass, whether it's for lack of knowing, lack of doing, or lack of persevering. Wherever you are, God has not changed His mind about His plan for you. You have a specific purpose, and that has not changed; it is not too late for you!

ENFORCING PURPOSE SECTION

At the end of the book, I have included many worksheets that I have used over the years with clients to help them move forward in their purpose. Each worksheet addresses a different aspect of working out your purpose, but they are all as useful as you want them to be. I am a firm believer in the importance of thinking things through and working things out. Too often, we don't learn something new because we think we already know it. The worksheets are designed to help you discover YOU.

Please do not dismiss them. Let them peel back the layers to your heart. Personally, I do these worksheets on an annual basis as I am kicking off the year, and every year, I discover something more about who I am and where I want to go.

ENFORCING YOU SECTIONS

As you move forward in enforcing your purpose, I urge you to recognize the importance of the intentional engagement of enforcing YOU. This is why I have included an Enforcing YOU section at the end of each chapter. They are much like those in my book *Enforcing You*. This involves reading a verse of scripture and then declaring it back to God as you reconcile that same Truth within your own heart. I recommended using a mirror as you state the self-reconciliations to yourself. This will help shift you from just believing what God says about you to actually speaking to yourself the way He does. We must retrain our self-talk!

Practicing your God-design must be a continuum in your life as you pursue purpose. In fact, it is the key to the "success" of enforcing your purpose. To the same degree that you discover and enforce YOU will be the same degree that you discover and enforce your purpose. This is not a once in a lifetime experience; it must be the way you live your life, persevering in enforcing YOU as you move on toward your purpose. So, with that in mind, let's dig in and start learning how to step into your purpose!

Chapter One
Designed to Prosper

OK, before you write off this chapter based on its title, do not assume what "prospering" does or does not mean based on what you know or what the world or religion would say. I want to really help you grasp an understanding of the mentality behind prospering. To do so, let's compare it to the mentality behind *not* prospering or what is called "poverty mentality."

God did not create us to think small or shrink back (see Hebrews 10:38). We are created to grow and increase; it is in our design. The Holy Spirit empowers us to live leaning forward, confident and assertively moving ahead, accomplishing and conquering life. After all, we are indeed called to be the "head and not the tail" (see Deuteronomy 28). But this has nothing to do with the world's definition of prosperity; it has everything to do with under-standing our position and possibilities in the Kingdom through Jesus. It is important that you understand that God has set you up to succeed in your purpose. You are designed to prosper.

UNDERSTANDING POVERTY

The mission of Crazy8 Ministries is "Attacking poverty, one person at a time." It is our desire to come alongside people who are "stuck" in life and help them move forward. Sometimes they are "stuck" because of their circumstances, sometimes it is because of their mental or emotional health, sometimes it is an unhealthy relationship, or sometimes it is simply because of their upbringing.

Often, it is a combination of all of it! Over the years of working in this field, I have learned a lot about poverty and how it really is a matter of the heart and mind. We see and experience the effects of poverty, but the root is unseen. Poverty lies deep within the individual, and the motive of the "poverty spirit" is to keep the person from moving forward. The enemy is so sly in that he will distract us through the circumstances of poverty to keep us from addressing the heart of poverty. We have learned that "resource without opportunity" doesn't work. In fact, it only perpetuates the cycle of poverty. One who is stuck in poverty needs to have things in the heart and mind addressed as well as stirred up for action. They must move beyond the anchors of their past and catch the wind of their future. This is why combining counseling with life coaching, when we are helping those in our housing programs move forward, is so imperative. The counseling reinforces who they are, while the coaching stirs up where they are going. Again, it is combining the concepts of enforcing YOU with enforcing PURPOSE, allowing them to work in tandem.

So, let's take a look at poverty. While there are many definitions of the term and many ways that the world might categorize it, I am interested in looking at it from a biblical perspective.

FRUITFULNESS AND MULTIPLICATION

The Truth is that we are designed to prosper. Look at this part of the very first blessing that God spoke over man during creation.

> *"God blessed them and said to them, "Be fruitful and increase in number; fill the earth and subdue it. Rule over the fish in the sea and the birds in the sky and over every living creature that moves on the ground." Genesis 1:28*

While I would love to write an entire book on the fullness of what we can learn through just this one verse of the blessing, for the sake of understanding poverty, I want to focus on the phrase, "Be fruitful and increase in number."

The word fruitful in Hebrew, "parah," actually means "to bear fruit." More specifically it means "to cause to bear fruit or to show fruitfulness." Don't miss what is implied. God's first blessing was to CAUSE man to bear fruit to the point of a display of fruit. In other words, "I have designed you to live a life that has evidence of growth."

I can't help but think of Isaiah 5, when Isaiah speaks of the parable of the vineyard that was planted on a fertile hillside. He says that all the rubble and weeds were cleared out and it was planted with the choicest vine. In other words, the vineyard was set up to produce fruit and prosper. He even goes on to say that a wine vat was positioned in the middle of the vineyard because there was an expectation of fruit! (see Isaiah 5:1&2) This is a parable about God's desire and intent for the children of Israel, more specifically, His desire for you and I as children of God. It was His design; the blueprint was to bear fruit. God has set us up to produce fruit and prosper to the point of already preparing in advance all that will be necessary for us to produce the finest wine. He set us up to succeed in life, to prosper and be productive!

But it gets even better! Going back to Genesis 1:28, take a closer look at the word "multiply." The Hebrew word for multiply is "rabah." It means "to become great or many, to become numerous or grow great; to make large, enlarge, increase greatly or exceedingly." It also denotes the idea of "to shoot." In my mind, I visualize something propelling forward with great force. So not only have we been designed to bear fruit, we are also designed to live a life that leans forward with great force into our futures with an increase of production as we move (to multiply).

In my book *Mastering Your Seasons*, I go into great detail on the design of a seed, and how we expect that it will not only produce fruit, but that it will produce MORE fruit with each year. We so easily embrace that design for a seed but hesitate to embrace that design for us, God's seed! Isn't it true that we have let our experiences in life define what should or could be true for us? To repeat the concept taught throughout my book *Enforcing You*, we too often let our reality define Truth instead of letting

Truth define our reality. Just because you have not experienced the fruitfulness and increase of life that God designed you for, that does not negate the existence of it.

Consider the Israelites in the wilderness. God had a promise of an abundance of fruit, milk, and honey in mind for them. It was the blessing He was moving them toward. But fear, doubt, unbelief, reasoning, etc. kept them from stepping into that promise. Although this resulted in them being stuck in the wilderness, IT DID NOT NEGATE THE ESTABLISHMENT OF THE PROMISE! Just on the other side of what they were experiencing was fruitfulness and increase. Yet there they were, wandering in the wilderness. Again, my point is, just because you may be experiencing a wilderness, that does not mean an establishment of growth in your life does not exist.

How does this connect with poverty? Some synonyms for the word poverty are deficit, famine, lack, scarcity, shortage, barrenness, beggary, impoverished, insufficiency, pauperism, or poorness. These are just a few, but you get the point. These words reflect the total opposite of our design. Yet I would venture to say that many of us live a life that looks more like poverty than it looks like our design. Hear me when I say that we are not just talking about poverty on the outside, but more importantly, on the inside. Remember that poverty starts in the head and the heart. In our program, we focus the entire first year on inward healing. Outward healing doesn't happen until closer to the second year because to deploy too quickly is foolish.

POVERTY MENTALITY

Attacking poverty is all about addressing what you believe about who you are designed to be and how you are designed to live in the fullness of your identity and your purpose. Remember the Israelites? They knew that God promised them a "land of abundance." They even SAW the evidence of that abundance when they brought back "clusters of grapes" (see Numbers 13), yet they wavered in their belief. They let the perception of being too small, too weak, and too insignificant navigate their decision to shrink back instead of letting the Truth of God's Word thrust them forward into the promise! They forgot their identity and got focused on their circumstance that seemed too big to conquer, thus they remained stuck in the wilderness. Hear me, God was trying to give them the resources, but their hearts and minds kept them from prospering. Therefore, their issue wasn't lack of resources; their issue was lack of confidence in their design. In other words, it had nothing to do with what they had and everything to do with reaping the fullness of their identity and the fullness of their purpose as God's children.

Many people ask me if I believe in the prosperity gospel. My response is, "Call it what you want, but what I know for sure is that I DON'T believe in a poverty gospel!" The Bible I read is all about God trying to move His people from a land of lack to a land of plenty, from a mindset of lack, to a mindset of abundance, from a life of not enough to a life of more than enough, from decrease to increase, from fruitless to productive, from death to life. Even scientifically, for something to be classified as living, it must grow and develop, use energy, and reproduce. This is the DNA of our design! In addition, God Himself IS a God of plenty, a God of abundance, and a God of increase. He is a God who is always producing... day after day, new stars are shooting forth into the universe, new buds are shooting up from the ground, and babies are being born! He is alive and ever-producing. This is WHO He is, a God of prosperity, and we are created in His likeness (see Genesis 1:26). This means we are designed to be like Him. This does not sound like poverty, but it DOES sound like prosperity.

> *"A thief has only one thing in mind—he wants to steal, slaughter, and destroy. But I have come to give you everything in abundance, more than you expect—life in its fullness until you overflow!" John 10:10*

This widely quoted verse certainly captures what we are talking about.

In our housing program, the first step to overcoming poverty is addressing the unbelief that growth, abundance, and life to the fullest are not only possible, but they are a part of our design. If we are honest, we aren't much different when we look past the outside. Many of us also don't move forward because we either don't know it is in our design to be fruitful and multiply or we simply don't believe it. Many of us are stuck as well, just maybe at a different place. Some are stuck in the past (Egypt) and some are stuck in fear or emotions (the wilderness), but anything less than the abundance and fruitfulness of His promise of freedom is poverty mentality. Again, this is way more than circumstantial.

This truth, that we are designed to overcome a poverty mentality and prosper, is important to enforcing your purpose because if you believe that it is God's design for you to be fruitful and multiply, then you will believe that it is also His desire for you. That said, let's be careful not to define prosperity the way the world does. To say that it is about money is to put God's idea for prosperity in a box.

PROSPERITY MENTALITY

The definition of prosperity is "a state of being prosperous," which denotes the idea of thriving with evidence. Isn't that what God said in Genesis 1:28? It is unfortunate that the world has convinced us that the only evidence of thriving is "stuff" or material things. Personally, I believe that prosperity is directly connected to the fulfillment of your identity and the fulfillment of purpose, not your pocket. Prosperity is experienced as your "God design" and "God purpose" is fulfilled. Your fullness IS His promise. That is YOUR promised land and your prosperity. It is being who He called you to be and pursuing the stirrings of your heart. It is living in victory and fulfilling the call that keeps you awake at night. Simply said, it is where you thrive! This is Kingdom prosperity and you must believe that God has this in mind for you. It is His desire and it is in your DNA. He designed you to be productive and FEEL productive, to thrive and live life leaning forward, shooting into your destiny. You are set up to succeed and designed to prosper!

I would be remiss if I did not include in this chapter the promise given to us in the first half of Deuteronomy 28. This chapter reveals to us the fullness of the blessings that God wants to "overtake" us with when we surrender to His ways and walk in His Word. Although it's a long text, it is worthy of reading to bring credence to the point of this chapter. As you read it, keep in mind that in every passage of Scripture, we learn something about who God is, His character, and His heart. We also learn something about the design of man and our "God-possibilities."

> *"Now it shall come to pass, if you diligently obey the voice of the LORD your God, to observe carefully all His commandments which I command you today, that the LORD your God will set you high above all nations of the earth.*
>
> *"And all these blessings shall come upon you and overtake you, because you obey the voice of the LORD your God:*
>
> *"Blessed shall you be in the city, and blessed*

shall you be in the country.

"Blessed shall be the fruit of your body, the produce of your ground and the increase of your herds, the increase of your cattle and the offspring of your flocks.

"Blessed shall be your basket and your kneading bowl.

"Blessed shall you be when you come in, and blessed shall you be when you go out.

"The LORD will cause your enemies who rise against you to be defeated before your face; they shall come out against you one way and flee before you seven ways.

"The LORD will command the blessing on you in your storehouses and in all to which you set your hand, and He will bless you in the land which the LORD your God is giving you.

"The LORD will establish you as a holy people to Himself, just as He has sworn to you, if you keep the commandments of the LORD your God and walk in His ways. Then all peoples of the earth shall see that you are called by the name of the LORD, and they shall be afraid of you. And the LORD will grant you plenty of goods, in the fruit of your body, in the increase of your

livestock, and in the produce of your ground, in the land of which the LORD swore to your fathers to give you. The LORD will open to you His good treasure, the heavens, to give the rain to your land in its season, and to bless all the work of your hand. You shall lend to many nations, but you shall not borrow. And the LORD will make you the head and not the tail; you shall be above only, and not be beneath, if you heed the commandments of the LORD your God, which I command you today, and are careful to observe them. So you shall not turn aside from any of the words which I command you this day, to the right or the left, to go after other gods to serve them."
Deuteronomy 28:1-14

Clearly, we learn that it is indeed God's heart to bless His children. It is in His nature to spoil us with goodness. It says that He will cause us to be fruitful and multiply... to prosper and be productive. This is God's character and His attitude toward His people. He WANTS us to live life abundantly. But we also learn that the design of man is to walk as ones who are blessed—productive and prosperously. We are created to be "the head and not the tail," meaning we are to have authority over our days and not be victimized by life. This is the opposite of living with poverty mentality!

It pleases God, "delights the Father," to "give you the kingdom," (see Luke 12:32). He finds great pleasure in blessing you and I. He designed us for it... to want it, to crave it, to seek it, and to pursue it. Unfortunately, many have confused the design of the spirit with the cravings of the flesh. The world has distorted the beauty of Kingdom prosperity with worldly riches. Now, I am not saying that Kingdom prosperity does not or should not include worldly riches, but what I AM saying is our motive should be for prosperity within us instead of around us.

I think you will find that as you read through Deuteronomy, your spirit will bear witness with what is being said. No matter your circumstances, no matter your mindset, there is a Kingdom narrative that is being spoken that should shake you up and cause a rising within you. That is the Spirit of God telling you that this is right, and you are designed to be overtaken with blessings. Yes, indeed! You are designed to believe and live productively. Consider honestly whether you could be missing out because your mind has settled in the land of "lack" or "just enough." Could there be more that God wants for you? Could there be more that God wants for you to do? Is your mindset keeping you from embracing a bigger, more prosperous possibility for you? Don't let the world's definition of prosperity be your narrative, but don't let religion be your narrative, either. Rather, let the Kingdom be your narrative and embrace that you are designed to prosper!

Prayer Practice:
God, thank You that You are re-writing my

understanding of what it means to prosper, to grow, and to live abundantly. I receive YOUR narrative, and I agree that I am designed to prosper. I thank You, Father, for shifting my mindset out of poverty and into the promises of a soul that soars by the Holy Spirit into a life that is prosperous and abundant. You have caused my life to overflow with Your Kingdom riches and the fullness of my inheritance in Christ. In Jesus' name I pray, amen.

Enforcing You

Verse:

> *"I am the vine, you are the branches. He who abides in Me, and I in him, bears much fruit; for without Me you can do nothing." John 15:5 NKJV*

> *"I am the Vine, you are the branches. When you're joined with me and I with you, the relation intimate and organic, the harvest is sure to be abundant. Separated, you can't produce a thing." John 15:5 The Message translation*

> *"I am the sprouting vine and you're my branches. As you live in union with me as your source, fruitfulness will stream from within you—but when you live separated from me you are powerless." John 15:5 The Passion translation*

Declaration:

God, I declare that as I stay connected to You, You cause me to bear fruit...not just a little bit of fruit, but MUCH fruit. An abundance of fruit! You have designed me to produce and prosper. The vine of Your love nourishes me and feeds me. My identity thrives as I abide in Your love. I declare that You have designed me to prosper and that You have empowered me for productivity. In Jesus' name I pray, amen.

Self-Reconciliation:

(Insert your name), you are designed to produce fruit and grow, to live a life that has the evidence of fruit. As you live in the abundance of His love, so you are experiencing the fullness of His fruit in your life. You sense His fruit on the inside, His character and His person growing within you daily. In this you are sure! You are living each day more abundantly because God designed you and blessed you to grow and multiply! In Jesus' name I pray, amen.

Chapter Two
Designed for Purpose

Purpose gives you your "why" in life; it is your quest, your journey. It thrusts you into your future. It transcends self and gives a sense that we exist for something outside of ourselves and beyond our today. It drives growth and imputes energy. Science will tell you that feeling a sense of purpose is a key to mental well-being, in fact, it is scientifically proven to ward off the effects of dementia.

We see the role of purpose evidenced biblically. From the very beginning of creation, God had a purpose in mind for man, i.e., a work for man to step into and fulfill. One of the first things that God did for man was to position him in the garden to tend it and keep it. God literally positioned Adam to fulfill a purpose.

> *"Then the LORD God took the man and put him in the Garden of Eden to tend and keep it."*
> *Genesis 2:15*

Now, I don't believe for a moment that God NEEDED Adam to take care of His garden. God created the garden and He is the Master Gardner. So, why was Adam invited into the tending of it? Although God didn't need Adam, He knew Adam needed a purpose. Without purpose, Adam would not have had a reason for living or any unction for life. God knew that Adam's work in the garden would bring him satisfaction and fill him with a sense of significance in the world. Adam's work proved his value. What is the point of life, if we bring no value? Adam's role in the garden was important to his own soul. It wasn't about the garden; it was about Adam's soul. It wasn't about producing fruit around him; it was about producing fruit within him. Isn't this the very definition of prosperity that we discussed in the previous chapter? Adam's well-being and wholeness, his prosperity and growth, hinged on working the work God designed him for. This was the fulfillment of his purpose.

Simply said, God designed man for purpose and without it, we feel empty, useless, and invaluable. But just like Adam's role was valuable to the growth of the garden, ours is valuable to the Kingdom.

It is the enemy's deception to keep you from working. He does not want you to know the value you bring nor does he want you to feel valuable. He wants you to feel stuck and useless, hence the poverty mentality. But God says that you have purpose. Not just any purpose, but a specific purpose that you were specifically designed for. Let's reflect back to *Enforcing You*. In that book, I wrote the following:

> *"'Eye has not seen, nor ear heard,*
> *Nor have entered into the heart of man*
> *The things which God has prepared for those*
> *who love Him.'*

But God has revealed them to us through His Spirit. For the Spirit searches all things, yes, the deep things of God." 1 Cor. 2:9-10 We are so good at quoting the first half of this passage and leave out the part about God letting us in on all He has prepared for us. Our purposes have entered our hearts via the Holy Spirit. God's Spirit is ever moving within us to open our eyes, open our ears, and stir up our hearts to the deep things He has in mind for us. This is our divine sense of purpose that is woven into our beings.

"He has made everything beautiful and appropriate in its time. He has also planted eternity [a sense of divine purpose] in the human heart [a mysterious longing which nothing under the sun can satisfy, except God]..." Ecc. 3:11a (Amplified Bible)

God plants purpose within the heart of every man. Moreover, that "God seed" contains the DNA to carry out that purpose. God Himself impresses the dreams that we dreamt as a child and the secret desires of our heart in us. And YOU, your flesh and your "person," are designed specifically and intentionally for that dream.

When God creates a human, I firmly believe that He starts with a purpose, a Kingdom assignment. He wraps that assignment in flesh, fills it with a personality (a soul) and then sends it to fulfill that assignment. Think about Jesus. God had a purpose, which was to save mankind, and He wrapped that purpose with flesh and sent Him to fulfill that purpose. It was a Kingdom assignment that was literally carried within the person of Jesus.

We see all throughout the Scriptures where someone receives a prophecy in regard to what assignment their child is going to carry out once the child is born. That prophetic word is speaking of the heavenly assignment that has purposed the conception, birth, and life of that child.

This should change the way we understand our value! We don't just have purpose; we have a SPECIFIC purpose that was prepared in advance to conquer. And God set us up for success in that purpose by designing and molding us around that purpose. In other words, YOU are perfectly designed for your purpose!

I couldn't have restated it any better than that. But now that we are looking at how to enforce our purpose, let's dive a little deeper into this concept of being designed not just with a purpose, but also FOR a purpose.

FASHIONED FOR PURPOSE

In Jeremiah 1, the Lord speaks to Jeremiah regarding his purpose. He starts by reassuring Jeremiah that his purpose has always been a part of him and that he was not chosen randomly. Rather, God was intentional in His Kingdom assignment for Jeremiah.

> *"The word of the LORD came to me, saying, 'Before I formed you in the womb I knew you, before you were born I set you apart; I appointed you as a prophet to the nations.'"*
> *Jeremiah 1:4&5*

There are several key words to focus on in this passage that will bring a greater understanding to how Jeremiah was purposed before he was born.

The word "formed" in Hebrew means "to form, fashion, frame, to be predetermined, be pre-ordained." It denotes the idea of this "fashioning" to be of "divine activity" or "of original creation." You were fashioned, formed, and pre-ordained by divine hands from the very beginning. The Message translation reads, *"Before I shaped you in the womb..."* capturing the idea of being sculpted, molded, or even manipulated by the Master's hands. This is why the Hebrew word is often actually translated into the word "potter" throughout Scripture. There is indeed a Master Potter who crafted you per HIS divine inspiration, and just as a cup is formed to fulfill its purpose, so you have been formed for your purpose. In fact, a cup is ONLY formed to fulfill its purpose. That is the only reason for its creation... to fulfill the role of holding liquid and providing drink, and it is unique in its design because it has a unique function.

When we, as humans, see a need in the world, we problem-solve for a solution. Marketing 101 says that to sell a product, we must prove the demand for that product. If there is no need, no one will buy it. So, the first thing we do is ask, "What makes this product valuable? What need does it satisfy?" We must answer these questions to expose the need to the buyer. In point, God sees the needs of humanity, and you and I are designed specifically to fulfill those needs. And just like a cup is fashioned to "be successful" in fulfilling its role, so we are fashioned to be successful in fulfilling our roles. He sets us up to succeed in accomplishing our purposes. You are adequately and perfectly suited to your purpose!

Let's move on to the next word I want to focus upon in this verse: "knew." The word comes from the Hebrew word "yada," which means much more than our understanding of "knowing something." This Hebrew word typically is used to express an intimate type of knowing. The definition includes "to ascertain by seeing, to comprehend, to perceive, to discern or discover." The word is used in a variety of senses, implicating a deeper knowing than what takes place in the mind. To give you a greater understanding of the depths of this word, it is the same Hebrew word that is used in Genesis 4:1, *"And Adam knew Eve his wife; and she conceived..."* In this verse, the word was actually used to denote the intimacy of sex. I think it is fair to say that this word implicates an intimacy of oneness. God is expressing the depths of how intimately He was acquainted with Jeremiah while He was fashioning him in his mother's womb. And so it is with you and I. I am profoundly "wowed" by the idea that God knew me on a more intimate level BEFORE I was born than I likely know myself at 47 years old. I find this idea wildly freeing and incredibly exciting. I find peace in the Truth that while there are things about myself I do not understand, there is nothing about me that stumps God. He is intimately aware. He comprehends my innermost being and knows me to the point of impregnating me with His works that are perfectly suited to my form.

This brings us to the next phrase in this verse, "I set you apart." Many translations of the Bible use the word "sanctified" or "dedicated" in this verse. The Message reads: *"I had holy plans for you,"* and The Voice reads: *"I had already chosen you."* No matter what version you read, we can conclude that God is communicating that there is a specific "something" that Jeremiah was designated for, set apart for, sanctified for, chosen for, dedicated for, and designed for. That "something" was his purpose. Let's sum this up in a self-declarative prayer practice:

"God, I thank You that I was fashioned perfectly and intentionally by Your hands while I was still in my mother's womb. Even BEFORE I knew life, You knew my life. Before I knew You, You knew me. I praise You that I can relax in the Truth that You have always been intimately acquainted with my plans and purposes and that You designed me to succeed in those plans. There is not a thing about me, God, that You don't know. There is nothing about me that is a mystery to You. You have set me apart, dedicated me to this purpose and I have been sanctified for it. I have not stumbled upon my purpose, I have been chosen for my purpose! In Jesus' name I pray, amen."

The last word in these verses that I want to look at is the word "appointed." I am not sure if we can quite grasp the depths of what it means to hear the voice of the Lord say, "You have been appointed." The word in Hebrew has many synonyms. Here are just a few: "To give, grant, ascribe, employ, designate, entrust, yield produce, be assigned." The Voice translates it like this: *"Before you drew your first breath, I had already chosen you."* I think we are starting to understand how this all points back to the truth that God placed His hand on each of us for a specific appointment; that we have all been designated for a specific something for which we will "yield produce." That "something" is your purpose, your work, and it was prepared for you long before you were born. It was the very reason you were created, and your design is perfectly suited to it!

> *"For we are His workmanship, created in Christ Jesus for good works, which God prepared beforehand that we should walk in them."*
> *Ephesians 2:10*

God created a work, and then He created the worker. Furthermore, He designed the worker for the work that he or she should accomplish it! The word workmanship here denotes the idea of a product, such as fabric, that is woven. We get the word "poem" from the Greek word "poiema." This goes back to God as The Potter or Author who fashions a product. In this case, He fashioned you and I for a work that was prepared beforehand. So, which came first? The work, the purpose, the intention, and then came the product.

GOD'S THOUGHTS TOWARD YOU

Let's look at another well-known verse.

> *"For I know the thoughts that I think toward you, says the Lord, thoughts of peace and not of evil, to give you a future and a hope."*
> *Jeremiah 29:11*

Understanding the Hebrew word for "thoughts" really helps to grasp what is being communicated in this verse even better. Its definition includes the words "plan, purpose,

27

imaginations, device, and invention." This is totally different from how we interpret the word "thoughts." God's thoughts about you and I are all about the plans for our lives, *His plans* for our lives. When He sees us, or thinks about us, His thoughts are in some sense "wrapped around" a specific purpose, a creative imagination or invention that is prepared just for us. Again, we are created FOR a specific "something" that is so much a part of who we are that it is included in the thoughts that God thinks toward us.

Furthermore, this verse goes on to say that those "thoughts, plans, and purposes" are for us, not against us. They are favorable and beneficial to who we are and what our lives entail. I think it is worthy to note that the word "peace" in this verse comes from the Hebrew word "shalom." This word encompasses not just peace, but the idea of wholeness, welfare, and prosperity. Remember, we are designed to prosper and walk in wholeness, to live productively and purposefully. That is what God reiterates in the verse. Listen to me, God has a future in mind for you, and that future is one that is filled with a purpose that produces. He has given you a hope, a hope that you were born with. The KJV reads that His plans are *"to give you an expected end."* Isn't that what hope is? A feeling of expectation, a desire for a specific something to actually happen? Good news, friends! God has given that to you!

I can honestly tell you that the loss of

purpose, the loss of vision, and the loss of a dream are directly connected to the loss of hope. When we don't feel a sense of purpose, we lose our unction for life. The forward lean gets stolen because we don't see the path set out for us to race. I see this continually in the counseling room. The loss of purpose equals a loss of life. No hope, no desire, no passion, no fire, no vision for tomorrow. Part of my goal through this book is to stir up purpose, but it is also to give you practical tools to pursue that purpose.

The Bible says in Proverbs 29:18 that people without revelation or vision perish, that they "cast off restraint" (my paraphrase). When we have no vision, or no revelation of our "God-purpose," what is there to strive toward? We will find ourselves lying around with no desire to move or get up ... with no direction or plans for our days. Remember Adam in the garden? He was given a work for this very reason. God wanted him to recognize that his life was valuable, that he had a purpose. This is by far the most difficult thing we have to overcome with the residents in our housing program. They have lost their dreams. Life has stolen, crushed, discouraged, and defeated them. But we know that the dream is still within them. Why? Because we know that we are ALL designed for purpose. We know that God knows the purpose He thinks toward them—a purpose that is intended to prosper them and give them hope! We cling to that Truth despite what we see and despite what they see. I will be delving into this verse later in the book, but for now, know that it supports the Truth that you are designed for purpose.

Grasp this: YOU were fashioned all around your purpose. This is why so many of us are on the search for our purpose, it is the "drive of God" within us to prosper and produce in life. I believe this is also why the Proverbs 31 woman "can laugh at the days to come" (see Prov. 31:25 NIV). She knows that all the days ordained for her are written in a book! She understands that her life is purposeful and filled with prosperity and productivity... life to the fullest!

I could go on and on citing Scripture to support the idea that you are designed for purpose. It is so important that you believe this before you move forward, otherwise doubt will keep you from enforcing your purpose. Don't allow what your life looks like now, or what it has looked like in the past, to define your Truth. Remember from *Enforcing You* we learned that your reality does not always equal your Truth. You MUST choose to believe God when He says, "I have designed you FOR purpose," not just ON purpose, but also FOR purpose. There is indeed a specific "something" within you, and I know that I know that you are set up to succeed in that "something."

Prayer Practice:

How exciting it is to know that You have created me intentionally and specifically for a Kingdom purpose... that my life holds incredible value to You. I relish in the idea that I was created for a work and that my design is perfectly suited to that work. Thank You, God, for putting in me a purpose...for putting in me a "reason" to get up every day and to live life leaning forward. I rejoice in knowing that my life is designed for Kingdom impact and You hold the plan in the palm of Your hand. In Jesus' name I pray, amen.

Enforcing You

Verse:

*"For we are His workmanship, created in Christ Jesus for good works, which God prepared beforehand that we should walk in them."
Ephesians 2:10*

Declaration:

God, I declare that You have crafted me perfectly for good works and that You prepared me, before I was even born, to succeed in all that You set me to do. I declare that I am YOUR workmanship, molded and fashioned by YOUR hand and that I am perfectly equipped to walk out my purpose.

Self-Reconciliation:

(Insert your name), you are crafted perfectly by the hand of God for a specific work. You are prepared and adequate because God has made you adequate. You will succeed in all that God calls you to because He is IN you and you are His! Walk confidently, knowing that you are His workmanship and that He knows your end from the beginning.

Chapter Three
Your Purpose, Your Dream

While most of us typically can connect with the concept of being created for purpose, personalizing that purpose is more of a challenge. Many of us go to bed at night pondering the question, "What is my purpose?" This is not unique to you; it is something that I deal with every day with the clients I serve. Again, sometimes knowing a Truth conceptually but not embracing it as a reality can be difficult.

In this chapter, we will take some time to look at dreams. Not just the dreams we have at night, but more so, the dreams in our hearts. Many people dismiss the dreams of the heart, assuming that they are nothing but high and lofty imaginations. To quote Cinderella, "A dream is a wish your heart makes." Dreams reflect the desires and wishes of the heart; they are the substance of your purpose. Hints of who you were created to be and what you were designed to do exist inside of your heart. Proverbs 27:19 says it like this:

"As in water face reflects face, So a man's heart reveals the man."

Tucked deep within you is a purpose, and the heart is where that purpose is stored and stirred.

The heart reveals not just who you are, but also what you are designed for. I believe this is why the Bible implores us to guard our hearts "above all else" because the heart is where God stores the plans and purposes of a man. It is the "wellspring" from which life in entirety flows and is supplied.

> "Above all else, guard your heart, for everything you do flows from it." Proverbs 4:23 NIV

The Message translation says it like this:

> "Keep vigilant watch over your heart; that's where life starts"

I think we too quickly dismiss or ignore what is in our hearts. This verse reminds us that our entire lives start within our own hearts. It is the seat of our emotions, passions, and aspirations. However, I fear that too many have learned that there is only wickedness in the heart. I know I heard Jeremiah 17:9 quoted many times as I was growing up: "The heart is deceitful above all things, and desperately wicked, who can know it?" (KJV) However, we must not take this out of the context of God's heart. To grasp a truer understanding of what God is saying here, let's read it in The Message version and include the verse right after it that is sadly often left out.

> *"The heart is hopelessly dark and deceitful, a puzzle that no one can figure out. But I, GOD, search the heart and examine the mind. I get to the heart of the human. I get to the root of things. I treat them as they really are, not as they pretend to be."*
> *Jeremiah 17:9&10 The Message translation*

OK, wow! There is definitely a huge "But" in this passage! "But I, God..." What we learn is that God sees that there is a difference between *who we are* and *how we behave*. God is saying that although man often behaves wickedly, He knows who we REALLY are. He goes to the root of our creation and treats us according to our "God-design" to draw out our God-possibilities. He knows that our hearts were designed for His love, His goodness, and His Kingdom. The heart indeed is a puzzle and it is hard to figure out, but each piece reflects the picture that God has in mind for us. We must not ignore the cries of our hearts! This is why our dreams are so important. They reveal the passions of the heart and the secrets of our lives. In our childhood dreams God stirred up the purpose we were designed for.

There are so many places throughout the Scriptures where God calls on the heart of man to allure him deeper into intimacy with Himself. He created the heart to speak to us, to stir us up, and to draw us into the path He has laid out for us. He sees the beauty of the heart and locks your purpose into it like one would lock up a jewel within a treasure box.

It should be guarded so closely because the enemy wants to steal what's in it! Satan does not want you to see the value of your purpose, the dream that is in your heart. He wants you to consider your dream as nothing more than a lofty, ridiculous wish that can never possibly come true.

The phrase "to dream" in Hebrew means "to be healthy, to be strong, to restore health." The primitive root means "to bind firmly." I am not sure that we have ever recognized the power of a dream and how having a dream plays a part in your health and wellness. The Hebrew definition reminds us that there is a direct correlation between dreaming and being healthy and strong. Let's face it, there is nothing worse than the loss of a dream. Think about the times you have experienced the disappointment of an unfulfilled dream—something you longed for, worked for, sacrificed for, given your life to—that failed. Maybe it was a business venture, maybe it was a relationship, or maybe it was your education or a sport. Whatever the case, the loss of what your heart was wishing for affects every part of your being. Our minds, our emotions, and even our physical health can be impacted by such a loss. Without a dream, we lose our perspective and sense of well-being—our purpose! "To bind firmly" implies that something is deeply rooted and firmly bound up in you. It suggests that to have a dream is to "attach yourself" to an imagination, a vision, and passion that navigates you to your destiny. The bottom line is that a dream becomes a part of you and brings life to your living. It is the substance of your purpose and reflects what God put in your heart when He knit you together.

In Genesis 37, we read about Joseph and the dreams that he had. The dreams were clearly a reflection of his "God-purpose" in that he would be the one who would rescue his family from famine... someday. There were hints about his purpose in his dreams. They were not just crazy, lofty, ridiculous aspirations, but rather they were the substance of his purpose being revealed to him, hints to where he was headed. His dreams began to navigate his life and steer him toward his purpose. And while I know Joseph had these dreams while he was sleeping, clearly he knew they were more than just dreams to be dismissed. So much so that he talked about them and shared them. I have no doubt that those dreams, although confusing and seemingly haughty, were brought to his mind frequently. Like Mary when she was told about the immaculate conception of Jesus, Joseph likely pondered the dreams in his heart.

There are many stories in Scripture that demonstrate someone having a "knowing in their knower" about their purpose. Hints in their hearts reflected what God had purposed them for from the very beginning. Consider Moses, who killed the Egyptian for beating up an Israelite long before he heard the call to rescue his people. I am in no way saying that God called Moses to kill the Egyptian, but I am saying that there was a passion in Moses's heart for the Israelites. That passion was a hint of his purpose. There was something in him that stirred up anger for the mistreatment of God's children. Moses, although born an Israelite, was raised as an Egyptian. He lived as an Egyptian, was groomed as an Egyptian, dressed and ate like an Egyptian, and he walked like an Egyptian (you're welcome, Bangles). Yet despite his system, there was something inside of him that rose in defense of the Israelites. We don't know if he knew his heritage, but something tells me that his heart knew his heritage. The God-purpose in him connected him to his future AND his past! That's amazing.

Or how about David, who showed up at the battlefield with bread and cheese for his brothers, but when he heard about Goliath, something stirred within him? I believe that was God's purpose within him, speaking to him through the heart, whispering that he was purposed to be a warrior!

My point here is that God is continually preparing us and stirring us for our purpose. There are hints of His path for you and I throughout our lives. His hand is ever-navigating us into fulfillment of our purpose and fullness of life!

> *"You will show me the path of life; In Your presence is fullness of joy; At Your right hand are pleasures forevermore." Psalm 16:11*

The Hebrew definition for the word "show" means "to make known, to distinguish, to perceive or discern, to become acquainted with." God Himself will distinguish our paths to each of us, personally.

Throughout our lives, He is ever revealing hints through our hearts, causing us to become acquainted with our purpose. But remember, we have an enemy who wants to keep us from that path. He knows that he cannot crush your life, so instead he will seek to crush your dreams. Remember, your dreams bring health to your being!

Let's go back to Joseph and his dreams. Joseph did not guard his dream well; he foolishly communicated his dreams to his jealous brothers. I am not saying that I might not have done the same thing, but I am saying that we can learn a lot from his experience. It is important to know that while we *should* talk about our dreams, we should be intentionally choosy about who we communicate them to.

When I was first catching a vision for Crazy8 Ministries, I shared some of the dreams that I had sensed in my heart. I was passionate for speaking and for helping people be set free. I was zealous, probably a little over-zealous, and began sharing with people that I wanted to write books, and be a speaker, and open a shelter, and start a counseling center, and, and, and, and ... I was like a puppy with really big paws who innocently causes damage when he is excited. It was not my intention to offend people or come off haughty or foolish, but there were some people with whom I simply should not have shared so much. I was wounded multiple times by responses that I received that were less than encouraging. I felt like Peter who was hearing God say, "Come, listen to my

39

voice and you will walk on water." But the message I got from many was more like, "Sit back down in the boat and don't rock it!" "Who do you think you are that you think you could walk on water?" Or a few less aggressive ones that were more like, "Well, if you think that is the Lord's will for you..." Not everyone was FOR my dreams.

Remember how David's brothers responded when he asked about fighting Goliath? Let me remind you.

> *"Then David spoke to the men who stood by him, saying, 'What shall be done for the man who kills this Philistine and takes away the reproach from Israel? For who is this uncircumcised Philistine, that he should defy the armies of the living God?'*
>
> *"And the people answered him in this manner, saying, 'So shall it be done for the man who kills him.'*
>
> *"Now Eliab his oldest brother heard when he spoke to the men; and Eliab's anger was aroused against David, and he said, 'Why did you come down here? And with whom have you left those few sheep in the wilderness? I know your pride and the insolence of your heart, for you have come down to see the battle.'"*
> *1 Samuel 17:26-28*

It's shocking that the people who should have

been in favor of David were the ones who came against him. His own brothers were aroused in anger and accused him of being prideful. Now, I am certainly not saying that this will always be the case when you share your dreams, but I am saying not to be shocked when it IS the case. Ultimately this is not about the brothers and their lack of support; this is about the enemy using those who are closest to David to snuff out his fire.

CONSPIRACY AGAINST YOUR DREAMS

The minute you begin to communicate your dreams, your passions, or even hints of where you think your life is headed, the enemy will begin scheming ways to steal it.

Like David, Joseph also received a less than encouraging response from his brothers regarding his dreams. In fact, the Bible says that they "conspired against him to kill him!"

> *"Now when they saw him afar off, even before he came near them, they conspired against him to kill him. Then they said to one another, 'Look, this dreamer is coming! Come therefore, let us now kill him and cast him into some pit; and we shall say, 'Some wild beast has devoured him.' We shall see what will become of his dreams!'" Genesis 37:18-20*

The definition of "conspire" includes the idea of working in secret to do an illegal or unlawful act, typically to someone's detriment. This is what Joseph's brothers were doing. They contrived a secret plan to destroy Joseph's future. I cannot think of a better picture than this when it comes to grasping an understanding of how the enemy works in our lives. He operates in the darkness, in secret, scheming and conspiring ways to keep you and I from our futures. He wants to steal, kill, and destroy us (see John 10:10). From the moment God formed you in your mother's womb, the enemy has been whispering, "We shall see what will become of your dreams!" Isn't that the message that we wrestle in our own minds? We wonder if our dreams could possibly come true. Do I have what it takes? Is this dream too big for me? What if this is just a lofty imagination? That is the conspiracy theory of the devil! He will do everything he can to discourage you, frustrate you, and weary you in the pursuit of your dreams because he does not want you to fulfill your purpose!

In the book of Ezra, King Cyrus, a pagan king, had his heart stirred to release the Israelites from captivity for the purpose of rebuilding the house of God in Jerusalem. It is interesting to note that although all the Israelites were invited to go back and rebuild, only some responded to the call. I don't really know, but from my perspective, I think it is fair to say that those who lost their identities as children of the One True God likely lost their purpose as well. They lost their vision for their Heavenly Kingdom and became content with the Babylonian kingdom instead. I see here a forfeit of who they were created to be and with that, a loss of purpose as the children of God. That said, the ones who responded went back to Jerusalem for the purpose of building the house of God. In Ezra 3, despite their fears, they erected an altar for the Lord and laid the foundation of the temple. Throughout all of this, they were stepping back into the practices of their heritage, giving offerings, praising, worshipping, dancing, etc., thus remembering who they were; they were Israelites! When you read this book, the first three chapters are filled with excitement and momentum. The remnant of the heart of Jerusalem is being resurrected! But then in chapter four, the enemy enters the scene.

> *"Then the people of the land tried to discourage the people of Judah. They troubled them in building, and hired counselors against them to frustrate their purpose all the days of Cyrus king of Persia, even until the reign of Darius king of Persia." Ezra 4:4&5*

Look at the words "discourage, troubled, frustrate." I think I can safely say that we are all-too familiar with those words. Yet they have nothing to do with God; they have everything to do with the conspiracy of the enemy. When fear couldn't steal their identity, discouragement, troubles, and frustration showed up to steal their purpose. The building of the temple came to a screeching halt and sat unfinished for 60 years. What a depiction of how the enemy works to bring our purpose to an end.

The word "discourage" here actually denotes the idea of a weakening of the hands. In fact, the KJV reads, "Then the people of the land weakened the hands of the people of Judah..." The Hebrew word for "weakened" means "to sink, relax, sink down, be disheartened, to let drop." We can all relate to the feeling of being discouraged and the feeling that everything inside of you is sinking or being "let down." It is experiencing disheartenment that causes one to feel, "I have lost heart, passion, and drive. I have lost sight of my purpose, my 'why,' and I am completely discouraged." This is what the enemy did to the Israelites... and it worked. The people of the land didn't touch them, beat them, or physically hurt them. Instead, they went after their hearts and frustrated their purpose.

The enemy knows the power of your dreams. He knows that they are the substance of your purpose and that they navigate you toward that purpose. Your dreams hint to what is in your heart, and the enemy will do anything to steal them. He wants to crush your heart, weaken you, and keep you from building anything in life. When he can't steal your identity, he will seek to steal your purpose to keep you from being effective in life— living less than in the fullness of your "God-possibilities."

Dreams are important to our being. Without them, we have no focal point, no direction, and we live aimlessly. The dictionary definition of the word dream is "a series of thoughts, images, and sensations occurring in a person's mind during sleep; a cherished aspiration, ambition, or ideal." Hey Cinderella, this isn't just a wish our heart makes while we're fast asleep; this is a wish our heart makes while we are awake! It is the cry of our heart that speaks in the night, but it also speaks during the day. It is the "something" we can't stop thinking about because it is so connected to who we are, our God-design. There is a difference between just having a dream and a dream having you. The dreams that are reflective of your God-purpose will not let go of you. No matter how much you try to shake it, it will continue to be an unnerving voice in your head, the stirring in your heart and a visual in your imagination. Over the years, you may have dampened it, quieted it, ignored it, and shut it down, but you know it is still there. You may have veered around it, settled for a different path, or run in the opposite direction, yet there is something that still causes you to wonder, "What if..."

This book is giving you your opportunity to dream again... to stir up the "What ifs" and courageously partner with God to release your heart's cry and begin to believe in your dreams again. Be free to put into action the steps it will take to move toward your "God-possibilities," your "God-potential," and enforce your purpose.

Prayer Practice:

God, thank You that You are the Chief Dreamer and that You have a dream about me. I relish in the dreams and considering their possibilities! I love to dream with You and ponder "could be's" of the Kingdom. Thank you for putting a dream inside of me and for teaching me how to dream. I rejoice in the cries of my heart knowing that they are evidence of what You put within me when I was still unformed. What a beautiful life You have blessed me with, and what beautiful dreams You have given me. Thank You, Father! In Jesus' name I pray, amen.

Enforcing You

Verse:

> *"Above all else, guard your heart, for everything you do flows from it."*
> *Proverbs 4:23 NIV*

Declaration:

God, Your Word says that ABOVE ALL ELSE, I should guard my heart and that I should be diligent in keeping a watch over what my heart contains. I thank You that inside of my heart, You have tucked my purpose. Thank You that my purpose comes flowing out in the forms of dreams and desires... reflecting the things You have designed me to be passionate about. I recognize the value of my heart surrendered to Your Spirit and that every step, every goal, every desire starts in my heart and flows from there. I submit my heart to You, and I give You the key. I declare that I will guard my heart and keep it pure before You. In Jesus' name I pray, amen.

Self-Reconciliation:

(Insert your name), you have a heart that is purposed by God. Your heart is filled with dreams and passions that reflect His purpose for your life. You have purpose, you have dreams, and your heart is full of His plan for you. You find the value and worth of what your heart contains, and you have no problem guarding what is dear to your purpose.

Chapter Four
Your Dream, Your Vision

From purpose to dreams, from dreams to vision!

We have spent some time understanding that we are all created with and for a specific purpose. We have come to understand that the dreams we too often dismiss are actually the substance of our purpose. Our aspirations hint to who we are designed to be and what we are designed to do. Dreams are the stirring of the heart crying out from inside of you trying to navigate you into your purpose. So how does vision connect with all of this? We hear a lot about the importance of having vision, so how does this tie in with all we have been discussing about purpose and dreams?

Let's recall the definition of the word dream: "a series of thoughts, images, and sensations occurring in a person's mind during sleep; a cherished aspiration, ambition, or ideal." The definition of the word vision is: "the faculty or state of being able to see; the ability to think about or plan the future with the imagination or wisdom." I like to say that dreams are of the heart, but visions are of the eye. If we add the Holy Spirit to the definition of vision, we might say it is "the faculty or state of being able to see what has only existed within your heart." A vision is in some regard "the next step" to a dream. While a dream is the substance of your purpose, a vision is the substance to your dream.

Hebrews 11:1 says:

"Now faith is the substance of things hoped for, the evidence of things not seen.

"Faith is the assurance of things you have hoped for, the absolute conviction that there are realities you've never seen."
The Voice translation

Let me sidestep for a moment and talk about the difference between hope and faith. Hope is "a feeling of expectation and desire for a certain thing to happen." It is a feeling. I like to say that hope is in the heart! Faith, on the other hand, is the substance of the hope... it is the next step. Faith shifts what is in the heart to the mind's eye, so we don't just feel or aspire for it, but we can actually see it! Faith is the shift from "I hope" to "I know." Dreams and visions also work in tandem. Dreams are in the heart; they are the stirrings of things you wish or want to come true. They are feelings and aspirations. But vision is the substance of those feelings and aspirations; it is the next step. Vision shifts dreams from what is hoped for in the heart to what the eye sees in the mind. Like faith, vision is the assurance of the dream you have hoped for, the absolute conviction that your dream is the reality of what God has put in your heart! It is the shift from "I wish" to "I see."

Ultimately, vision is the ability to see your purpose coming to pass. It is seeing yourself in the role of fulfilling your God-purpose. It is more than just a dream; it is your dream played out in your mind. Therefore, your vision SHOULD be the expression of your purpose. So let me pause here for a moment and tell you that this is where a lot of people miss it. Too often we focus on vision before we focus on purpose. Somehow, we have adopted the understanding that vision will lead us to purpose when it is actually the opposite. It all starts with knowing YOU. The more you know who you are, the more you will come to know your purpose. Your purpose will stir up dreams and ultimately bring vision to your life.

JESUS, THE VISION CASTER

When I read the gospels, I marvel at how well Jesus told stories. For example, He would say, "The Kingdom of heaven is like..." and then use ordinary things, objects, and people in hopes of giving His listeners a visual model for something they had never seen. He used their earthly frame of reference to connect with them in order to draw them into another frame of reference, the Kingdom of Heaven. It was almost as if He was saying, "Imagine a world like this..." Tapping into their mind's eye, He stirred their imaginations to captivate them and draw them through Narnia's door, into a world that was indescribable and incomprehensible. He used visuals to help them see that there was a reality, a Truth, that existed beyond what their natural eye had ever seen. He casted the vision for what years of prophecy had spoken of; bringing substance to what had been unseen (see Heb. 11:1). He gave eyes to what was in their hearts, the hope of another Kingdom that would supersede what they had always known. Jesus was not only the Master Storyteller, He was the Master Vision Caster. Jesus knew that vision stirred imagination. This was the next step. Jesus shifted their dreams into visions, stirring up their purpose as children of God.

GOD, THE VISION CASTER

In Genesis 12, God revealed Abram's purpose to him, which was that God would make him "into a great nation."

> *"I will make you into a great nation,*
> *and I will bless you;*
> *I will make your name great,*
> *and you will be a blessing.*
> *I will bless those who bless you,*
> *and whoever curses you I will curse;*
> *and all peoples on earth*
> *will be blessed through you."*
> *Genesis 12:2&3*

I can't help but wonder how often Abram had pondered these words in his heart. No doubt he would dream of this, both while sleeping and awake.

To hear the voice of God speak His plan for your life is to awaken the heart to your purpose. From there, the heart cries out, reminding you through dreams and aspirations of what should be and could be for you.

Then, in Genesis 13, God gave Abraham a glimpse through his eyes as to what that purpose LOOKED LIKE. Furthermore, He invited Abram to define the magnitude of it.

> *"Lift your eyes now and look from the place where you are—northward, southward, eastward, and westward; for all the land which you see I give to you and your descendants forever." Genesis 13:14&15*

Notice that God did not say, "The land I am showing you is what I will give you..." Instead He says, "For all the land which YOU see I give to you..." (emphasis mine). God uses Abraham's eyes not only to show him what he could literally see, but also to consider what could be. He invited Abraham to imagine more, to see beyond the natural and press into the supernatural. He stirred up his God-potential. Just like Jesus did in the gospels, God started with what Abraham could see, then pulled him beyond the boundaries of possibilities. Only instead of casting the vision for him, God invited Abraham to cast the vision for the dreams in his heart. It was as if God said, "How much do you believe Me for? How much demand will you put on

My Word?" There was a subtle message that said, "To the degree that you are willing to see, is the degree that you will BE."

Let's look at another example in Jeremiah. God also uses the eye to give Jeremiah a taste of what his Kingdom purpose is. Watch the progression of how God starts by confirming Jeremiah's identity (Enforcing YOU), then speaks his purpose, and then moves to vision.

> "Then the word of the LORD came to me,
> saying: 'Before I formed you in the womb I
> knew you; Before you were born I sanctified
> you; I ordained you a prophet to the nations.'

> "Then said I: 'Ah, Lord GOD! Behold, I cannot
> speak, for I am a youth.'

> "But the LORD said to me: 'Do not say, 'I am a
> youth,' For you shall go to all to whom I send
> you, And whatever I command you, you shall
> speak.

> "Do not be afraid of their faces, For I am with
> you to deliver you,' says the LORD.

> "Then the LORD put forth His hand and
> touched my mouth, and the LORD said to me:
> 'Behold, I have put My words in your mouth.

> "See, I have this day set you over the nations

and over the kingdoms,

"To root out and to pull down, To destroy and to throw down, To build and to plant.'

"Moreover the word of the LORD came to me, saying, 'Jeremiah, what do you see?' And I said, 'I see a branch of an almond tree.' Then the LORD said to me, 'You have seen well, for I am ready to perform My word.' And the word of the LORD came to me the second time, saying, 'What do you see?' And I said, 'I see a boiling pot, and it is facing away from the north.'" Jeremiah 1:4-13

The Bible doesn't say whether or not Jeremiah physically saw the branch of an almond tree in nature, but I believe we can fairly assume from context that this entire exchange of words, touch, and vision was likely a spiritual encounter (especially if you include the vision of the boiling pot in verse 13). Whether it was of the natural eye or the spiritual eye, God spoke a purpose and then confirmed the purpose through the eye. The vision shifts what God had put within Jeremiah since he was in the womb from the heart to the eye. I believe that God did more than give Jeremiah a word, I believe He proved Jeremiah's purpose to him.

I think it is worth noting that the Hebrew word for "almond" in verse 11 and the Hebrew word for "perform" in verse 12 is "shaqad." Yes, they are the same word in Hebrew! The word means "to wake, watch, be alert, to keep watch, to be wakeful." Jeremiah knew that an almond tree buds before any leaves show on the tree, often as early as January, thus meaning it "awakens" earlier than other trees. The almond was watched to determine the first signs that spring was coming. Again, we see that God used the natural to give a visual for the supernatural. The vision was an analogy to explain and bring understanding of how His word works. In this case, the almond branch is like the Word that "goes before" and speaks to what is coming.

There are layers to what God showed Jeremiah, but my point is that God knows the importance of vision in regard to purpose. God used a vision to disciple Jeremiah in the ways of a prophet and how prophesy works. He brought understanding to Jeremiah's purpose. I don't want to chase a rabbit trail too much here but know that Jeremiah's purpose started with vision. Again, God knows that to the degree that we can see will be the degree that we will be.

THE SCIENCE CONNECTION

Science will tell us that everything we do first begins as a thought. Every action, every word, everything that we produce exists first in our imagination. The ability to see things before they happen is what enables us to pursue our dreams and ultimately achieve them. Visualizing is the powerful next step that shifts you from dreaming to seeing.

When my daughter was in gymnastics, the coaches would have the kids visualize their routines in their minds... over and over. There were times when she would turn on the music to her routine and just sit with her eyes closed, while she ran through every motion in her mind. Furthermore, she visualized herself sticking every landing, nailing every move, and succeeding! This was a regular practice for them. If they were having a hard time sticking a landing, their coach would have them step aside to spend time visualizing "a perfect landing" in their minds. It was amazing how much it made a difference. This is the power of visualizing!

The brain cannot differentiate well between real action and mental action. Research has shown that visualizing an action will fire the neural pathways in your brain just as if you were actually physically doing the action. Many Olympic gold medalists have testified to using visualization techniques, visualizing both the action and the emotion tied to winning! I know that as a life coach, I use visualization with my clients to help them see the fruit or outcome that they have only been "dreaming about." I want them to see themselves already "on the other side." But I also want them to connect with who they would be and how they would feel. They connect by visualizing in the mind.

VISION BRINGS LIFE

Having vision is imperative because we cannot

obtain what the eye does not first see in the mind.

"Without a vision, the people perish..."
Proverbs 29:18

The word "perish" in Hebrew means "to let go, to loosen, ignore, let alone, neglect, avoid, show lack of restraint." It denotes the idea of letting go of the reins and living life unbridled. In other words, to perish means to live without intention or without direction. This verse instructs that vision is a focal point that reminds us of our purpose and therefore gives us unction. We automatically navigate toward what the eye is looking at. In the next chapter, we will talk specifically about the *power* of vision, but suffice it to say that this verse connects vision to how we live. Will we live life aimlessly or will we live it with clear direction? Will we be navigated BY life, or will we navigate our life?

When I hear the word perish, I connect it with death or extreme suffering; it is a loss of life. To perish ultimately means to die. That sounds a bit extreme when talking about the importance of vision, but is it? We have talked a lot about the idea of prosperity and living life to the fullest, fulfilling your purpose. I have shown that you are designed to grow, produce, and prosper. God tells us in this verse that having vision is a key component to the fulfillment of our purpose and that without it, we will experience a "loss of living."

VISION EXPRESSES PURPOSE

Recall that at the heart of your vision is your purpose. This is important to remember as we move forward in establishing vision. It should absolutely point back to your purpose; it should be an *expression* of your purpose. This means that if I were to look at your vision, I would learn something about what is in your heart, what you desire, and what drives you or "trips your trigger." Purpose and vision go hand-in-hand in that they stir each other up. Keeping your eye on your vision stirs up your purpose, and your purpose stirs up vision. Your purpose is in your core, it is a part of who you are, and it is in your design. Your vision is the expression of that purpose. It brings what is hidden in your heart out into the light, revealing your secret passions and desires.

I work with people all the time who are what I call "idea people." They have lots of really good ideas and think that they should pursue them all. They end up spending a lot of time and energy chasing the wind of ideas instead of their purpose. Not every idea or vision in your head is for you to pursue. If it isn't connected to who you are, if it doesn't reflect YOU, then it may be nothing but an idea, albeit good or not. Part of my job as a life coach is to help my clients figure out which visions are the expressions of their heart. This is where the question, "What is the desire of your heart?" comes in. It is amazing to me how many people have great ideas, but they cannot answer that question. The Psalmist reminds us that as we discover who we are in Christ, we will discover the desires of our heart.

> *"Delight yourself in the Lord and He will grant you the desire of your heart." Psalm 34:7*

The problem is that we too often delight ourselves in things, people, ideas, ventures, and even dreams more than we delight ourselves in GOD. That is dangerous and will fill our hearts with "worldly delights" and false hope. Our deepest-seated desires are found as we delight ourselves in God. This again is the whole purpose of *Enforcing YOU*. Delighting in God and delighting in your design will stir up your purpose and ultimately will release HIS vision for your life.

Prayer Practice:

God, I rejoice in the gift of sight! Thank You, Lord, for giving me the ability to not just see what is around me, but to see within myself. I am amazed at the beauty of the mind's eye and the power You have given me to see by Your Spirit. Release my mind's eye, Lord. Show me more... more of You, more of me, and more what You have for me to do. I declare that You are opening my spiritual eyes to see my kingdom purpose for Your glory and Your name! In Jesus' name I pray, amen.

Enforcing You

Verse:

> "Without a vision, the people perish..."
> Proverbs 29:18

Declaration:

God, I declare that having vision fills me with joy and life. I call You a God of Vision, The Vision Giver, and the God Who Stirs up Dreams. I declare and decree that Your vision for my life causes me to lean forward and puts breath in my lungs. You have given me a reason to leap out of bed and run into my tomorrow. I have life because I have vision! In Jesus' name I pray, amen.

Self- Reconciliation:

(Insert your name), you have vision. Your eyes see your possibilities in the Spirit and Your heart is stirred by what you see. There is no fear of the days to come, instead you rejoice in considering your future. You are confident in God's vision for you and you have excitement in life because of it!

Chapter Five
The Power of Purpose

Having purpose plays a powerful part of living more fully and intentionally. I have personally learned how staying connected to my purpose keeps my imagination stirred up and active. My purpose energizes me, keeps me running my race, and motivates me to never give up. It also has helped me establish my priorities. Imagination, motivation, and priorities are each important components to living a strong, vivacious life with clear direction and purpose. Purpose empowers you to live imaginatively, motivated, and with clear "purposed priorities." Let's delve into these power points of purpose.

IMAGINATION

The definition of imagination is: "The act or power of forming a mental image of something not present to the senses or never before wholly perceived in reality." Simply said, the imagination is the ability of the mind to be creative or resourceful. To imagine is to form a mental image in the mind's eye; it is to picture something in your head.

As children, we used our imaginations all the time. In school we were given assignments, work-sheets, coloring books, art activities, projects, and more to activate and stir up the imagination. Yet, as adults, we have lost the art of imagining. In fact, I would say that we even fear imagining things outside of what we can see, explain, or comprehend. The imagination requires creativity, which, by the way, is a biological drive. However, since creativity requires freedom and no fear of failure, somewhere between childhood and adulthood, creativity gets squelched, and we lose touch with our imagination!

As believers, our imaginations get a bad rap a lot of times. It might even be called the devil's playground, where "no good takes place." I can honestly say that I have always had a strong imagination, but when I was in my mid-twenties, I heard a preacher once preach on the evil of the imagination. Quite honestly, he scared the life out of me as he emphasized the importance of "shutting off the imagination." I think the years that followed were some of my dreariest years, as I lost any kind of hope for something more in my life. I won't say that this was the cause of the clinical depression that I wrestled with, but I will definitely say that in closing my mind's eye, I lost vision for my future. No vision meant no dreams, no unction, no passion, no hope, and no purpose. Years later, as I was coming to know the Holy Spirit more powerfully and intimately, I started seeing things when I would pray. I would try to shut it down, thinking it was demonic interference of some sort. But the more I prayed and exposed myself to the prophetic gifts of the Spirit, the more I began to realize that God was using my mind's eye to show me things and navigate my prayers and my life. During that time of my life, I heard someone say that the imagination is God's writing tablet. The minute I heard that, the fear that I had agreed with years before was immediately broken and my imagination was set free to soar by the Spirit. Now, I do want to say that the imagination *can be* a breeding ground for evil; however, it is a part of our creation, therefore we can know confidently that its intention is for our good and for God's glory. But like every part of our body, we must surrender it to God and NOT the flesh.

> *"I beseech you therefore, brethren, by the mercies of God, that you present your bodies a living sacrifice, holy, acceptable to God, which is your reasonable service. And do not be conformed to this world, but be transformed by the renewing of your mind, that you may prove what is that good and acceptable and perfect will of God." Romans 12:1&2*

We hear this passage often, so don't skim over it and miss a valuable point. Read it again, specifically as it relates to the imagination. Every part of your body and mind is designed to discern God's will. God created us that way because He wants us to know Him and know His path for our lives. Therefore, God has given us what we need in order that we might know what He finds good and acceptable. He wants to reveal to us "the perfect will of God!" This design includes our imagination.

But we must surrender our imagination to the hand of God and allow Him to navigate it. My point here is that our imagination plays a valuable role in our purpose for the Kingdom. This is where our future begins... in the mind's eye.

Through your imagination, God gives you a visual of what your dreams look like so you can see what you look like fulfilling your purpose. It is His permission to stir up your passions through the mind's eye. When I am assigning a client to begin to consider what their purpose and dream looks like, I ask them to sit with the Holy Spirit and ask God to write on the tablet of their imagination. Sometimes I call it "intentional daydreaming." It is more than just mind-wandering, it is allowing the Holy Spirit to show you things, pictures, encounters, and experiences in your mind.

From a brain-function perspective, imagining requires the use of multiple lobes of the brain. Without getting too deep into this, I want you to grasp the beauty of what happens in the brain during the imagination process. I believe understanding it can help when intentionally exercising your own imagination. Both the visual and sensory regions are activated when imagination is in use, under the navigation of the prefrontal lobe (PFC). The PFC is affectionately called the "executive control center" of the brain. It keeps us focused, attentive, and engaged. This is important to note in the imagination process because it is the "turning on" of the PFC that distinguishes imagining from simply daydreaming or aimless mind-wandering. This is different from just staring out the window mindlessly. Using the imagination is one of the ways to exercise multiple parts of the brain at one time; therefore, it is good for your brain health.

From a spiritual perspective, the Holy Spirit keeps our minds on track with what He has purposed for us. Much like the PFC, it is imperative to "turn up" or engage the Holy Spirit when we are imagining our futures. I like to imagine dials in my mind where I picture my hand "turning down" my intellect and reasoning and "turning up" the Holy Spirit. I try not to think, but to imagine through the navigation of the Holy Spirit. This requires a lot of conversation and interaction with God as I seek to see what doesn't exist, yet is established in the Spirit. It takes practice, but this is crucial to enforcing your purpose. I have included a worksheet at the end of this book called the "One Year Narrative." This worksheet will require active and intentional imagining.

MOTIVATION

I want to spend quite a bit of time in this chapter talking about motivation. There is nothing more frustrating than wanting more, but not being motivated. I mean, have you ever tried to kick start yourself when feeling completely unmotivated? Let's press in and see if we can gain a greater understanding of how our purpose empowers motivation.

The definition of motivation is: "the act or process of giving someone a reason for doing something, the condition of being eager to act or work, a force or influence that causes someone to do something." Let me sum that up by saying, "Motivation is having a reason, being eager, and having a cause." This is where your purpose empowers you as the source of motivation! It becomes your reason, it is what makes you eager in life, and it gives you a cause. Your purpose is your "why." It is the force and the influence that compels you and motivates you; it is what gets you out of bed every morning and energizes you to attack the day. Staying connected to your purpose is imperative to feeling motivated. In other words, how connected you are to your purpose directly affects how motivated you will feel.

In my work as a life coach, any time a client sets a goal, it is important to identify "the why" behind the goal. This is to help the client to connect with the purpose of the goal. I might ask, "Why are we doing what we are doing?" or "Why is this essential to where you are heading?" or "How does this goal help move you forward to where you want to be?" These questions are to help identify the purpose behind the goal, thus ultimately motivating the client. Doing this exposes why it is imperative that they accomplish what otherwise might seem unnecessary, irrelevant, or too difficult. I want to fix their eye on what is set out in front of them and stir up energy and excitement to complete their goals.

We see this concept throughout Scriptures as well. Paul, in 1 Corinthians, says we should run with the intent to win; the intent to "obtain a prize." He says that a runner does not run "aimlessly" but is directed and motivated by the finish line. It is the finish line, completing the race, or more specifically, winning the race that motivates a runner to discipline his body. It is WHY he gets up every day and trains for months or even years. It is all about that finish line (see 1 Corinthians 9:24-27). Your purpose is YOUR finish line! It is what you are running for, training for, reaching for, and working toward. If you take your eye off the purpose, you will lose your desire to "train."

Even Jesus was motivated by His finish line.

> *"Therefore we also, since we are surrounded by so great a cloud of witnesses, let us lay aside every weight, and the sin which so easily ensnares us, and let us run with endurance the race that is set before us, looking unto Jesus, the author and finisher of our faith, who for the joy that was set before Him endured the cross, despising the shame, and has sat down at the right hand of the throne of God."*
> *Hebrews 12:1&2*

Jesus gives us the ultimate example of what it looks like to "run with endurance" and stay motivated, especially amid challenges and trials. He demonstrated the importance of staying fixed on the finish line because He knew it was the finish that would motivate Him and keep Him trudging ahead. Let's face it, life is hard, and if we don't keep our eye set on the prize, we will lose motivation and our strength to run will wane. That is the power of purpose; it stirs up motivation!

Let's look deeper at motivation to distinguish between intrinsic and extrinsic motivation. Simply said, intrinsic motivation comes from the inside. It is the natural stirring within a man to "do something." Intrinsic motivation is what makes things "easy." In other words, we are naturally, or intrinsically, motivated to do the things we love. Moreover, these things typically come easy for us and they bring us joy. They do not drain us; they energize us and motivate us to do even more. We don't need to be bribed, rewarded, or coerced to do these things because the reward is internal. We feel good, we feel accomplished, and we notice these things "come easy" for us.

We are all born with intrinsic motivation. For example, hunger drives you to eat, thirst drives you to drink, and fatigue drives you to sleep. When you eat, drink, or sleep, the reward is that you feel better, more satisfied, and content. The same is true in regard to other areas in each person's life. Whether it is cleaning, exercising, writing, gardening... we all have areas where we are intrinsically motivated. What intrinsically motivates me is not the same as what intrinsically motivates you. I point this out because the enemy will try to steal your motivation by saying things like, "You're just not a very motivated person" or "You have no drive." While it is true people are motivated by different things, it is simply not true that any one person could not be motivated at all. For example, I am not motivated to work on our budget at work, but I am motivated to counsel our residents. I lack motivation in cleaning my house, but I am always eager to sit down and write in my book. In other words, I am intrinsically motivated in the things that are connected to my purpose and I don't have to be coerced to do them. In this, I do have to stay connected to my dreams.

Conversely, extrinsic motivation is when action is driven by external things. These external things can be positive or negative. Rewards can motivate, but so can negative consequences. For example, if you are motivated to eat healthy because you don't want to gain weight, that is extrinsic motivation. If you are motivated to work harder at your job because you want a bonus, that bonus is an extrinsic motivation. Extrinsic motivation is often referred to as "sticks and carrots." The problem is that a person can be conditioned to only respond when sticks and carrots are present. This can lead to the inability to self-motivate. These are the people who need continuous affirmation, instruction, or even a bonus structure. They thrive on results and external rewards. They often have a hard time working autonomously because they aren't "self-starters." They tend to need acknowledgement, praise, or rewards to stay motivated in accomplishing their work.

Extrinsic motivation is not only based on external things, but also tends to be navigated more by the desires of the flesh or emotion than by the Spirit. In other words, I am motivated by how I feel as opposed to what I know. While our emotions can be great "energizers" that aid in propelling us forward, they should not be what navigates us. We are to be navigated by the Spirit, not by our emotions. Again, emotions make us passionate about what we are doing, but should not be our *source* of motivation. If it is, we will waver in our purpose based on feelings and current outcomes. This is so important to understand. When we base our purpose on emotions, we will not maintain our course and our motivation will waver with our emotions. As a speaker, I want to remember that although there is a purpose to stirring up emotional inspiration, I must go deeper. Yes, I want my audience to walk away feeling inspired, but also being empowered. I want them to feel confident in their purpose and potential. I do this by going beyond emotion and tapping into the spirit. This can be done even in secular settings just by talking about what is in the heart of man: purpose. This is an example of tapping into intrinsic motivation versus extrinsic motivation or just "emotional inspiration." I recognize that we are all designed with intrinsic motivation. But if that is the case, why don't we all feel intrinsically motivated all the time?

I think it is obvious that everyone wants to be intrinsically motivated. Here's some good news, knowing that you have purpose will do that. You may not necessarily know what your purpose is, you just need to be convinced that you have purpose! As believers, there is an internal force that compels us and stirs us to live focused on something that is beyond "self." This force causes us to work "heartily as unto the Lord" (see Colossians 3:23). This internal force is His presence and His promise that our reward is not on the outside, it is found on the inside. This force is His love. And the more we are convinced of His love, His plan, and His purpose for our lives, the more we are compelled intrinsically, and also spiritually.

> *"For it is Christ's love that fuels our passion*
> *and motivates us, because we are absolutely*
> *convinced that he has given his life for all of us.*
> *This means all died with him, 15 so that those*
> *who live should no longer live self-absorbed*
> *lives but lives that are poured out for him—the*
> *one who died for us and now lives again."*
> *2 Corinthians 5:14&15 The Passion translation*

Our reward is no longer what we see on the outside, but what we know on the inside; it is no longer driven by the flesh, but by the Spirit. The confidence of His love and His purpose for our lives will intrinsically motivate us, by the Spirit. The reward of His pleasure, His smile, and His nod—the affirmations of the Lord and the joy we get in running for Him—compels us. We no longer live focused on what is seen, but rather on what is unseen.

> *"So no wonder we don't give up. For even though our outer person gradually wears out, our inner being is renewed every single day. We view our slight, short-lived troubles in the light of eternity. We see our difficulties as the substance that produces for us an eternal, weighty glory far beyond all comparison, because we don't focus our attention on what is seen but on what is unseen. For what is seen is temporary, but the unseen realm is eternal."*
> *2 Corinthians 4:16-18 The Passion translation*

This verse captures the force behind what intrinsically motivates believers. We do the right thing for the pleasure of our King. We find joy in obeying His Word and following His plan. When we do, we recognize the "rewards" of heeding His call. The external rewards are often the outcome, but they should not be your motive. Paul says in Philippians 2:13: "It is God who works in you both to will and to do for His good pleasure." To will means "to WANT to do." In other words, I am intrinsically motivated only by the reward of His good pleasure. You see, God doesn't just put a purpose in your heart, He puts a "want into your wanter." Stay connected to God's purpose for you, and HE will motivate you to see it through! You must be confident in knowing that God will indeed bring you to your finish line... you just need to keep running!

> *"Being confident of this very thing, that He who has begun a good work in you will complete it until the day of Jesus Christ." Philippians 1:6*

PRIORITIES

When you prioritize, it means you designate or treat something as more important than other things. Ultimately, your purpose should drive your priorities. That is another empowerment of purpose. Too often, however, that is not the case. Let's be honest, we often end up prioritizing other things... most often things that seem more urgent, necessary, or important in a moment. And while sometimes those things really must be dealt with, most of the time, they are simply things that we just get sucked into. We end up victimized by our circumstances and allow ourselves to be navigated by everything around us. This leads to disorder and chaos, where we have no sense of authority of our own lives. I know you get what I am talking about; those days when you wake up with your "set list" ready to go, but then everything gets derailed because of the happenings around you. Minute by minute goes by and the next thing you know, your day is gone. And then one day after another goes by, and the next thing you know, your week is gone, and the month is gone, and the year is gone. Until you wake up one day and wonder what happened to your life, what happened to your dream, what happened to YOU?!

We will prioritize that which we value. When you don't see the value in something, it is hard to prioritize it. That said, oftentimes we don't prioritize our purpose because we simply don't see the value in it. Therefore, we put our purpose on the back burner and we end up living with no "purposed priority." Furthermore, instead of choosing our priorities, our so-called priorities end up choosing us.

I have had to reconcile in my own heart the value or the worth of my purpose. Having six children and a thriving ministry can often "steal the show" in my life, and if I am not intentional to guard what GOD put in my heart, I will allow everything else to be priority number 1! Hear me when I say that this is not about prioritizing YOU, it is about prioritizing what God has put IN you. Saying that my purpose is not urgent, necessary, and important is to deny the worth and value of my God-purpose.

Enforcing your purpose requires purposed priorities. In other words, setting intentional priorities that say, "I recognize I have purpose, AND I value my purpose." I realize there are different seasons for pursuing and prioritizing different things, but somewhere in there, you should find YOUR purpose, YOUR passions, and YOUR dreams.

You may not even know it, but when you prioritize according to what God has put in your heart for each season, you will begin to recognize how He is navigating your path to your purpose, one priority at a time.

When my kids were all still very small, I felt a need to study Scripture every day. When I say "need," I mean I had a deep stirring and a strong desire, and the study I felt called to was more than just the ordinary "quiet time." I felt this urge to the point of recognizing that there was a spiritual invitation that I needed to heed the call to. So I put a plan in motion to study daily. Well, in a house of six children, all being homeschooled, and having a husband who worked out of town, my plan was derailed day after day. I began to feel angry with my children (and with my husband), when the reality was I simply didn't know how to set my own boundaries to guard my own desire. Digging a little deeper, I began to realize that the stirring of my heart wasn't just my desire, it was God's preparation for where He would be taking me. BUT... would I believe that He had a purpose for me beyond my home? More importantly, did I value that purpose? Needless to say, I had to recognize the tolerances that I was allowing to interfere with my purposed priorities. The worksheet at the back of this book called "What are your Tolerances?" will be helpful for you in this area. I had to set boundaries and learn to prioritize "me." Here was the difficult part: I had no idea WHAT my "final" purpose was at the time. I had no idea that God was actually using that study time to prepare me to write books, messages, trainings, and more. All I knew was that I needed to prioritize that time and to do that, I had to see the value in that time!

The same is true of many of the things God asked me to value while I was raising my children and running a household. Things that not necessarily every mom does, like chore charts, goal setting, a daily routine, and regular Bible reading. It would have been easy to deem those things as unnecessary, but the Holy Spirit would speak things that I needed to prioritize. Little did I know that the things He called me to prioritize were not just about my home, but God was training me to run a housing program with many people and many children. My home was the priority of that season that was navigating my path more and more toward my purpose beyond my home.

> *"But seek first his kingdom and his*
> *righteousness, and all these things will be given*
> *to you as well." Matthew 6:33*

Many of us are familiar with this verse, yet do we REALLY grasp what is being said? What does it mean to "seek God's kingdom first"? What does that look like? Many of us are challenged enough by the idea of seeking God's kingdom and what that entails, but what about the word "first?" Does this mean that I must have my quiet time the minute I wake up every day?

To understand more intimately what this verse teaches, let's first take a look at it within the context of the whole passage.

"Therefore I tell you, do not worry about your life, what you will eat or drink; or about your body, what you will wear. Is not life more than food, and the body more than clothes? Look at the birds of the air; they do not sow or reap or store away in barns, and yet your heavenly Father feeds them. Are you not much more valuable than they? Can any one of you by worrying add a single hour to your life?

"And why do you worry about clothes? See how the flowers of the field grow. They do not labor or spin. Yet I tell you that not even Solomon in all his splendor was dressed like one of these. If that is how God clothes the grass of the field, which is here today and tomorrow is thrown into the fire, will he not much more clothe you—you of little faith? So do not worry, saying, 'What shall we eat?' or 'What shall we drink?' or 'What shall we wear?' For the pagans run after all these things, and your heavenly Father knows that you need them.

"But seek first his kingdom and his righteousness, and all these things will be given to you as well. Therefore do not worry about

79

tomorrow, for tomorrow will worry about
itself. Each day has enough trouble of its own."
Matthew 6:25-34

The overall theme of these full verses is addressing man's worries and anxieties about life. Let's face it, life is filled with unknowns and things we simply cannot control. Most of us try to appease the fear through control. The problem is that we end up prioritizing the things we THINK are going to keep us "safe." We work more to keep our jobs stable, we exercise more to keep our weight stable, we compromise more to keep relationships stable, and we get up earlier to get more done. Our nature is to prioritize what we feel will make us FEEL better. These things don't necessarily help us LIVE better. At best, they help us manage our days, but we never move forward and find solace, only temporary relief. Isn't it true that we seek a schedule that makes us feel accomplished? Isn't it true that we seek things that make us feel more secure? Isn't it true that we rely on "things" to keep our lives in order and at peace? This self-reliant thinking will leave you feeling anxious and worried because you are depending on YOU instead of on God! Note that verse 32 says, "For the pagans run after all these things..." What are your "things?" You know, the "things" that you seek to find a sense of fulfillment and peace. The worksheet called "Identifying the Things in your Life" will help you in this area.

God reminds us to seek Him and His Kingdom

first in all we do. He knows that our tendency is to try everything else before we seek Him. It is in our nature to seek order and what we call "life balance." But I think "life balance" is a façade that will keep us continually moving things around, adjusting our schedule, our attention, and our energies in the empty hope of finding balance. The Truth in this verse gives us the key to "life balance."

Read the verse again.

> *"But seek first his kingdom and his righteousness, and all these things will be given to you as well." Matthew 6:33*

Balance means we will pour equal parts into every area of our lives. However, this verse tells us the only things we need to prioritize pouring into are God and His Kingdom. The word "first" in this passage denotes the idea of rank. It is not just about time, it includes succession. Who or what is first in rank in your life? When we pour into our "God bucket" first, it becomes what we pour out of. For example, if every area of our lives is like a bucket that requires water, and we focus on pouring out of ourselves into each bucket equally, we will run out of water. But when we pour into our "God bucket" first, then He directs the filling of our "life buckets." Moreover, He will navigate you to the right buckets at the right times, and He will instruct on how much to pour into each bucket. Those are the "things" that God addresses in Matthew 6:33. He will add to the "things" as you prioritize Him. He knows what is important, and more importantly, He knows what is important to you. He has your best interest in mind, and He is aware of all the important things in your heart. Life balance isn't at all about equal parts, rather, it is about understanding how to let God prioritize for us in each and every season.

Let's bring this back around to purpose. It is hard to prioritize our own purpose when we are not filtering our energy first and foremost into God. He is the one who will stir up passion for where He is taking you. As you pour into Him first, He will organically tap into your heart, your purpose, and cause you to prioritize according to His plan for your life. This is the power of the purpose in your heart. It will keep you from being distracted by all the "urgencies" of life that keep you from fulfilling your purpose.

Solomon said it like this...

> *"Let your eyes look straight ahead,*
> *And your eyelids look right before you.*
> *Ponder the path of your feet,*
> *And let all your ways be established.*
> *Do not turn to the right or the left;*
> *Remove your foot from evil." Proverbs 4:25-27*

Keep your eyes on God first, and HE will establish your priorities. The Passion translation reads this way:

"Set your gaze on the path before you.
With fixed purpose, looking straight ahead,
ignore life's distractions.
Watch where you're going!
Stick to the path of truth,
and the road will be safe and smooth before you.
Don't allow yourself to be sidetracked for even a
moment or take the detour that leads to
darkness."

Now that is powerful! It is OK to prioritize your path of truth. Let God show you how to fit it all in because there is always enough time, energy, and resources to do the will of God. If HE purposed it in you, He will supply all you need to bring that purpose to fruition as you stay connected to Him in all you do...first!

In Haggai 1, the prophet finds the people of God tending to the needs of their own lives instead of building the temple of God. They were released from captivity (see Ezra 1) for the purpose of rebuilding the temple, yet they were found building their own houses instead. They did not prioritize their purpose. Read for yourself the results that followed.

"Then the word of the LORD came by Haggai the
prophet, saying, 'Is it time for you yourselves to
dwell in your paneled houses, and this temple to
lie in ruins?' Now therefore, thus says the LORD
of hosts: 'Consider your ways!'
'You have sown much, and bring in little;

83

You eat, but do not have enough;
You drink, but you are not filled with drink;
You clothe yourselves, but no one is warm;
And he who earns wages,
Earns wages to put into a bag with holes.'
Thus says the LORD of hosts: 'Consider your
ways!'" Haggai 1:3-7

I read this and think to myself … Yes, I have felt that weariness! The frustration of working hard, but still being "empty." Like hamsters on wheels, we think the answer is working harder, when in reality, most of us just need to reposition ourselves and prioritize according to our Kingdom purpose. The prophet goes on to say:

"Go up to the mountains and bring wood and
build the temple, that I may take pleasure in it
and be glorified," says the LORD. "You looked for
much, but indeed it came to little; and when you
brought it home, I blew it away. Why?" says the
LORD of hosts. "Because of My house that is in
ruins, while every one of you runs to his own
house." Haggai 1:8&9

In other words, go back to God and get the resources He has provided for you to do His work. Your energy will wear out, but God's won't; your resources will run out, but God's won't. The enemy will blow away the works of your flesh, but the works of the Spirit will always prevail! Some of us need to consider our ways and go back to our secret places to reprioritize our energies and provisions. Some of us need to consider who or what we are putting first that is leaving us exhausted and depleted.

Consider your ways! The Message translation says it like this: "Take a good hard look at your life. Think it over." The Israelites were in the middle of a drought that left them working hard, yet thirsty... all because they had forgotten their purpose. Are you thirsty? Are you experiencing a spiritual drought? Perhaps you need to consider your ways and return to His purpose for your life!

CONCLUSION

This was a long chapter, I know! But it is imperative that you understand how powerful purpose is. Imagination, motivation, and priorities are each important components to living a strong, vivacious life that is filled with joy and passion. Your purpose is the power source behind those things. As you stay connected to your purpose, you will indeed experience a stirring of your imagination, you will feel the internal motivation of the spirit, and you will find your priorities in perfect "God balance." It won't happen in the reverse. Press into God and what He has put in your heart FIRST, start enforcing purpose, and He will release your imagination, motivation, and purposed priorities into your life.

Prayer Practice:

I leap inside, God, at the reminder of how powerful my purpose is. Thank You for putting everything I need INSIDE of me to passionately run towards my Kingdom call. Thank You for giving me a forward lean that keeps me running my race. Thank You for prioritizing my life and for organizing all "the things" so that I rest well. I feel accomplished and it is well with my soul! In Jesus' name I pray, amen.

Enforcing You

Verse:

"Being confident of this very thing, that He who has begun a good work in you will complete it until the day of Jesus Christ..." Philippians 1:6

Declaration:

I declare that I am confident in Your promise to complete all that You started in my life. Just as You planted the seed of purpose inside of me, You will cause it to grow. I believe You and I trust You to see it through! I rebuke any doubt because MY God is faithful!

Self-Reconciliation:

(Insert your name), you are filled with confidence that God is working to complete all the desires and passions He's put inside of you. You are sure of what God has told you and you know He will see you through. You have no doubts and no fears. God's power and confidence are in you. You trust God implicitly and you know that He is good and faithful.

Chapter Six
Discovering and Defining your Purpose

We move now into the more practical side of enforcing purpose in our lives. The first step in moving toward your purpose is to have your purpose well-defined. I believe that is why the Bible tells us in the book of Habakkuk to write "the vision" down. As a life coach, I ask my clients to take what they know in their minds and write it down. This exercise may seem unnecessary, but it is imperative. Writing things down helps define what you DO know, and it also helps to reveal what you THINK you know but aren't sure of. We will talk more about writing down your purpose in a minute, but first, we can't go any further without discussing what is probably bothering many of you at this point. That is: "What if I have no idea what my purpose in life is?" You may not even be at a place to define your purpose because you have yet to discover your purpose. I almost wrote a whole chapter devoted to just discovering your purpose, but part of the discovery is in the defining process. You probably know more than you think you do about your purpose. I also believe that sometimes we wait to define until we fully know, and that will not likely happen. Like life, we discover as we go… the key is to watch with expectation for revelations of purpose in each moment. There are hints of what God is doing in you and through you in every moment of the day. You may not see it, but you must believe it. God is always at work and He is always navigating toward your Kingdom call!

DISCOVERING YOUR PURPOSE

What is the key to discovering your purpose? Simply said, the key is seeking God. Like I stated above, we must watch and expect God to reveal. This first requires the belief that you are indeed created for purpose and that God is for you in regard to accomplishing your purpose. Second, remember that your purpose is tucked inside of you. God has woven your purpose into your personality, your desires, your gifts, and your passions. Some of the worksheets at the back of this book simply ask questions to help you discover YOU! But the key to finding you is resting in God's presence. He wants you to discover your purpose, He wants to reveal it to you!

> *"Call to Me, and I will answer you, and show you great and mighty things, which you do not know." Jeremiah 33:3*

Let me demonstrate a declaration based on this promise...

> *God, You say that if I call upon You that You will not only answer me, but that You will SHOW me*

things... things that are big and mighty and outside my understanding and comprehension. I declare that I am seeking You now, I am calling upon You and I thank You that Your word is true. I declare that You are opening my eyes to see Your purpose for my life. Bypass my mind, Lord, and reveal Your path!

This Truth is also expressed by Paul in 1 Corinthians 2:9&10.

"But as it is written:
'Eye has not seen, nor ear heard,
Nor have entered into the heart of man
The things which God has prepared for those who love Him.'
But God has revealed them to us through His Spirit."

God has revealed to you and I all that He has prepared to do by His Spirit. These are things that are not revealed by natural sight or natural hearing, but by the Spirit of God. There are indeed hints in the natural, but revelation comes ONLY by the Spirit. So again, we hear a promise in this passage... declare it with me!

God, You say that there are indeed things prepared for me to do in this life and that by Your Spirit I will know them. I shift my eyes and ears to You, that I may see and hear what You have to say about all you have put in my heart. I desire to fulfill all You have prepared for me and I declare the spiritual revelation in Jesus' name!

Read it in The Passion translation!

"This is why the Scriptures say:
Things never discovered or heard of before,
things beyond our ability to imagine— these
are the many things God has in store for all his
lovers.

"But God now unveils these profound realities
to us by the Spirit. Yes, he has revealed to us his
inmost heart and deepest mysteries through
the Holy Spirit, who constantly explores all
things."

Not knowing your purpose and how to define it doesn't mean you don't have one, it more likely means you have been looking to discover or define it with your own mind or reasoning. Seeking your purpose only with your intellect will limit what you see. Conversely, seeking through the Spirit will open up the "great and mighty things, which you do not know," meaning it is unknown to your natural mind. I cannot tell you how many times I meet with coaching clients and as they start to really seek God, suddenly they have huge, audacious ideas and visions about where they want to go. I can honestly say it is 100% of the time bigger than they imagined!

"Never doubt God's mighty power to work in you and accomplish all this. He will achieve infinitely more than your greatest request, your most unbelievable dream, and exceed your wildest imagination! He will outdo them all, for his miraculous power constantly energizes you."
Ephesians 3:20 The Passion translation

We learn over and over that not only should we expect to discover, but we should also expect to discover something bigger than "life." In other words, your purpose is bigger than you think. It is outside of your natural capacity. If you have a dream that you have figured out how to achieve, I guarantee you it is not big enough. If you want to step into your spiritual purpose, you have to come to the end of "your natural." Your dream should frighten you in that it requires supernatural interventions from God! I like to tell my clients that when Lazarus was resurrected, there was the natural work of the disciples—rolling away the stone—but then there was the supernatural work of God—the raising of the dead. You will know you are dreaming big enough when you can see that the fruition of it will require this kind of partnership with God. There will be a natural work for you to do, but a supernatural work will also be required.

Take a moment and ask yourself, "Is my dream big enough? Does it require a miracle? Do I absolutely have to rely on God to see it through, or can this be something that I COULD accomplish on my own strength?

When setting goals, we want to stretch ourselves outside of our comfort zone. This is true when discovering your purpose as well. While our purpose is a good fit for us, thinking about it should feel slightly uncomfortable because we know it is outside of our own natural abilities. Your purpose should be "a stretch" for you, thus requiring you to lean on and depend on the Holy Spirit to see you through it.

Remember Gideon? God cut his army from 32,000 men to 300 men so that Israel would KNOW that it was not man's strength that saved them (see Judges 7:2). Defeating the enemy with 32,000 men was naturally possible, but defeating the enemy with only 300 men was supernatural!

Many of you haven't discovered your purpose yet because you won't let yourself dream outside your natural possibilities. You look at yourself as small and limited, and therefore you have limited yourself to something small and insignificant. This is part of why defining your purpose is so important... it releases the process of discovery!

So when seeking to discover your purpose, start with Who you know. God! Then remember what you know; God has designed you on purpose, with purpose, and for a purpose. Seeking God is an adventure of great discovery. Not only will you find out more about Him, you will find out more about you. As a life coach, I continually ask my clients what they are discovering about God, but I also want them to self-discover. I ask questions like: "What did you discover about you this week? What did you discover about you through that relationship? What did you discover about you when you were working on that goal? What did you discover about you in the middle of that conflict?"

While every situation is an opportunity to discover something about God, it is also an opportunity to discover something about you. I expect that as my clients seek God in regard to their purpose, they will discover things about themselves. As we discover who we are, we will discover what we are called to do! Remember your purpose will spill out of WHO you are. This is why I have included the Enforcing YOU sections at the end of each chapter. I want you to recognize that the discovery process of your God-design is a continuum; therefore, so is the process of discovering your purpose. The more you discover you, the more you will discover your purpose.

If you don't know your purpose, relax! Stop looking around you and look within you to God. Expect that He will reveal "all that He has prepared for you" (see 1 Corinthians 2:10) by the Holy Spirit. Remember, your purpose is tucked within you.

"Delight yourself also in the LORD,
And He shall give you the desires of your heart."
Psalm 37:4

A desire is a strong feeling of wanting to have something. The word in Hebrew means "to petition" and it denotes the idea of a craving. We are all born with internal desires, things that we crave. We talked about the "cry of the heart." This could also be called the "petitions of the heart." I like to phrase it "the tugging of the heart" or what your heart is "begging of you." Ask any child about the desires of his heart, and he will not have a problem telling you. Somewhere along the path of life, however, we start to squelch and ignore those desires. We get tired of wanting, waiting, never getting, and feeling disappointed. So we learn to suppress the desires of the heart. We rationalize them through reasoning and reality until we become numb to the desire. When residents first move in to our housing program, we ask them what the desire of their heart is and most of the time they can't answer. They have lost touch with the longing of their hearts because life has stolen their passion. Know that desire gives way to internal drive and motivation; we seek to discover what is hidden inside of their hearts. We often ask, "When you were a child, what did you dream about doing as an adult?" or "If you had no barriers and the sky was the limit, what would you be doing in life?" These two questions often start the process of cracking the wall that is around their hearts and shattering the hopelessness of having no purpose. We all have desires in our hearts; they are part of our design. Psalm 37:4 tells us that the key to releasing them is simply delighting in the Lord!

The word "delight" in that verse in the Hebrew language denotes the idea of being soft, delicate, or pliable. I can't help but think about a potter with clay. The clay starts out as just a soft lump. Whatever the potter wants to make of the lump, he can, as long as the clay is soft and pliable. It is a delicate process as the potter's wheel spins. Every point of pressure is intentionally shaping the lump into a vessel for a specific purpose. Some are shaped to hold water, some are shaped to pour water, some are shaped to hold soup, and some are shaped to carry a steak. Ultimately, the purpose of the vessel determines the shape of the vessel, and the potter has the purpose of the vessel continually in mind. But it can only be molded when it is soft!

So it is with us. As the wheel of life spins us round and round, God has His hand on our lives and is using every turn to shape our lives for a specific purpose. To the degree that we are pliable and soft in His hands is the degree that He can shape us and mold us. This is what it means to delight in the Lord. It means, "I am going to stay tucked in the palm of Your hand, Lord, and allow You to mold me how You want. I surrender my heart and my life to You!" This is how we not only get the desires of our hearts met, but also how we LEARN the desires of our hearts. God Himself will reveal to us the purposes of our lives through the molding process. This is the self-discovery process at work. Each point of pressure is a "hint" of what

God is doing and where He is taking us. Each point of pressure in life is intentional and important to the final outcome, which is also the desire of our hearts. The key is to stay surrendered in the hands of the Master Potter!

God has promised us that as we seek Him, we will discover all that He has planned for us. The enemy will try to discourage you from persisting in your seeking because he wants you to feel worthless and without purpose.

> *"Ask, and the gift is yours. Seek, and you'll discover. Knock, and the door will be opened for you. For every persistent one will get what he asks for. Every persistent seeker will discover what he longs for. And everyone who knocks persistently will one day find an open door." Matthew 7:7&8 The Passion translation*

We must persist in seeking His will for our lives; don't give up! Know that God WILL reveal the longing of your heart... expect Him to open the door and show you what is "behind the curtain." But ready your heart! Be ready to say, "Yes!" Be ready to be challenged and be ready to "do it afraid." Although your purpose will be bigger than you, know that you are perfectly designed for it. Remember, the Potter had your purpose in mind when He designed you. The bottom line is: GOD HAS NOT SET YOU UP TO FAIL! He will not call you to something that you are not empowered to fulfill.

Reread Ephesians 3:20.

> *"Never doubt God's mighty power to work in you and accomplish all this. He will achieve infinitely more than your greatest request, your most unbelievable dream, and exceed your wildest imagination! He will outdo them all, for his miraculous power constantly energizes you." Ephesians 3:20 The Passion translation*

Read that first sentence again and again until your heart and mind are in total agreement. Let His Word confirm any doubts and chase out any fears that are lurking in your heart or mind.

DEFINING YOUR PURPOSE

To define something is to clearly say what something is. This can be tricky when we are dealing with the idea of purpose, since we don't necessarily know specifically what our purpose "means" or "looks like." In other words, you and I can have the same purpose, but what it looks like can be very different. Moreover, my purpose can look one way for a season, but look another way in another season. This is why the dreaming and imagination process that was discussed in the earlier chapters is so important in defining our purpose and why we must practice it all the days of our lives. It is what pulls our desires from the heart into the mind's eye! Remember, purpose and dreams are of the heart, but vision is of the eye. Vision brings definition to your purpose and says, "This is what it looks like."

By sitting in the presence of God and allowing the Holy Spirit to navigate the mind's eye, we will receive vision for the purpose. Recall the story of Moses and how the blueprints for the tabernacle came out of his interaction with God on the mountaintop. Just like Moses, God wants to reveal the blueprints for our purpose as we sit with Him in the Spirit. These blueprints are the vision.

Think about when a homebuilder meets with a customer. They listen to what is in the customer's heart: the desires for their home, the needs of their home, and the PURPOSE that the home will fulfill. A good homebuilder will sit with you and try to capture all that you desire for a home in order to capture it and put it on paper for you to see. These are the blueprints for the home. Until there are blueprints, there is no vision. The homebuilder's job is to take the concept and put it on paper so the customer can see what their home will look like. This process is imperative to the building process.

> "Write the vision
> And make it plain on tablets,
> That he may run who reads it." Habakkuk 2:2

God also reiterates the importance of blueprints; the importance of capturing what is in your heart and putting it on paper. This can be a frightening step for many reasons, but it cannot be skipped! No matter how "dumb" your vision feels, or how unnecessary this step seems, defining your purpose starts by writing down what you see or envision in your mind! Though everyone is born with a dream, not everyone has a clear vision. A dream is something that you want to do. Writing it down says, "This is something I have *decided* to do!" It is an act of faith that says, "I believe You, God." Writing it down requires courage and unction and is a step that the enemy does not want you to take. He doesn't mind you dreaming, as long as you don't take action, in which case your purpose is just a fleeting dream in your heart that has no substance, no blueprints.

The blueprints are what make the vision "plain." In other words, they clearly communicate visually what is going to be done. The Hebrew word means "to make plain, to make clear, to make distinction, to engrave." Figuratively it means to explain or declare. The same reason it is important to write your vision down is the same reason you often fear it. It communicates clearly what you intend to do; it is a declaration of the plan, which carries some sense of accountability. It is one thing to have a list of things in your mind that you desire to accomplish; it is another thing to write the list down. We call this a "to do" list, meaning, this is what I intend TO DO! The list is a visual declaration that clearly states what I intend and holds me accountable to doing it. I don't know about you, but some of the desires and visions I have had in the Spirit are HUGE and I get a little freaked about writing it down for others to plainly see! My life coach requires this of me every year... to write down my visions for the year, and he always encourages me to think BIG! That document becomes my blueprint that clearly communicates my desires for the year. BUT it also comes with a sense of accountability that keeps me relying on God to help me accomplish all that He has put in me to do.

Writing down the vision is the bullseye that navigates us and keep us on task. It reveals what we are aiming for and reminds us of the bigger picture in our daily goals. We will talk about setting and accomplishing goals in the next chapter, but let it be said that keeping the vision in front of you helps to keep you motivated to accomplish your goals.

We also write down the vision and make it plain so that we can run with it! I can't move forward when I don't know where I am going. In other words, I can't run with what I am not sure of. A clearly communicated vision can be implemented. This is Leadership 101. A team can't accomplish a mission if they don't know what the mission is. This is why vision and mission statements exist, to give the people a target that keeps them motivated and moving collaboratively in the same direction. I can't help but recall Nehemiah and how he searched the land to assess what needed to be done to rebuild the walls of Jerusalem so that he could clearly communicate the building plan to the people. Nehemiah's purpose was to rebuild the walls of Jerusalem, but that purpose shifted from his heart to his eye as he intentionally scoped out the land with God. Only then did he have the vision that could be shared with the people (see Nehemiah 2).

A written-down vision will keep you running YOUR race. Again, it is the bullseye that keeps you on target and the blueprint that reminds you of what you are building. It keeps you on your path. As a life coach, once we determine the vision, from there my job is to keep my clients on task. There are many paths out there, but only one that is marked out for you.

> *"Therefore we also, since we are surrounded by so great a cloud of witnesses, let us lay aside every weight, and the sin which so easily ensnares us, and let us run with endurance the race that is set before us." Hebrews 12:1*

Don't be distracted by the path of emotions, the path of culture, or the path of others. Keep in mind that the world will try to suck you in through comparison and envy. Social media is a huge snare when it comes to this. There is a perception that the world presents that is deceptive and exhausting and we cannot allow it to pull us out of our lane. Those paths will ensnare you and keep you from running as freely and as swiftly as God has in mind for you. Be quick to throw those things aside! Turn off your phone and go back to your secret place with God. Recall what He has revealed to you about YOUR lane and write it down again and again. Writing your vision down will keep you on the path that God has purposed you for so that you can run with passion and determination.

In the book of Ecclesiastes, Solomon says that running the wrong path is like a "chasing of the wind." It will leave you ever-running but never finding, working but never achieving. Looking to the people around us is a chasing of the wind and will surely disappoint. Stop looking side-to-side and look up. Remember not just WHAT you are running for, but WHO you are running for. God must be your "why."

> *"Yet there is no end to all his labors,*
> *Nor is his eye satisfied with riches.*
> *But he never asks,*
> *'For whom do I toil and deprive myself of*
> *good?'*
> *This also is vanity and a grave misfortune."*
> *Ecclesiastes 4:8*

Chasing other paths leads to great exhaustion with no satisfaction. I have no doubt we have all experienced the feeling of "running in vain" at some point in our lives. Sometimes it is just a feeling based on the weariness of not seeing results, but many times it is because we are running the wrong path. It is only our God-purpose, clearly defined through a vision plainly written that will keep us running with intention and direction. No more exhaustion, no more running in vain; stick to HIS blueprints for your life.

Know that you might not get the whole picture as you start the defining process. This is why discovering and defining go hand-in-hand. Remember, writing it down is an act of faith. This can be because you are writing down something that seems ridiculous, but more often it is because you are sure of what you are writing down and you don't have all the answers. Start with what you know, and trust that God will reveal what else you need to know—as you go! Listen, you can know nothing, but if you know God, you know everything. Trust Him as you go. Write things down as they are revealed. Don't wait for all the details, God will fill them in at just the right times. In other words, as you discover, write it down, and as you write things down, you will discover more. This process NEVER ends. God will continually expand your purpose until you reach eternity. If you are not dead, He is not done. So never stop seeking Him for what He has called you to do and who He has called you to be, in and out of every season of life. Rest in His heart and you will always discover more and more purpose for your life.

CONCLUSION

There are lots of practical ways to help you discover and define your purpose. For example, taking personality tests or spiritual gifts tests can be very helpful when searching for your purpose. I am a HUGE fan of these kinds of tests, and while I use them and highly recommend them, they cannot and should not replace the voice of God. I believe that God will indeed use them to help you discover what makes you tick and what ticks you off, but do not allow such tests to define WHO you are. Don't let your personality-type box define who you are. Only God can define you. Not a single one of us fits into any personality type 100% because we are all uniquely created. Let the tests help describe you and explain you, but never define you or excuse you.

There are many worksheets included at the end of this book to get your spiritual juices flowing, but it is so important to remember to relax through the discovery process. Be patient and wait on God! Here is one thing I can tell you, when you start honing on the bullseye, you will know it. Your heart will shift from, "I have a dream," to "This dream now has me."

Finally, I want to remind you that it isn't so much about the path you are on as it is about who you are while you are on the path. God doesn't bless inanimate objects, He blesses people; so, it isn't about finding the "right" path, it's about being the "right" person while you are on the path. This is why the Psalmist was confident when he said, "SURELY, goodness and mercy will follow me ALL the days of my life" (see Psalm 23, emphasis mine). How did he know that? How could he be sure? I mean, he didn't even know all the paths of life he had yet to take. The reason he was sure was because he was sure of who he was and who he had decided to be all the days of his life. Therefore, he knew that because of who he was, God would cause him to be blessed and goodness and mercy would follow him on ANY path.

Sometimes we stress out too much on making sure we make the right choices, pick the right job, choose the right house, go to the right school, pick the perfect major, etc. The chance of you picking everything spot-on in line with God's perfect will is zero-to-none. And that's OK! God doesn't bless choices; He blesses people who make choices. Relax… don't focus on where you are going as much as who you are "while you are going." Focus on God and who you are in Him, and your purpose will flow from that confidence. It will be easy because it's perfectly suited for YOU!

Prayer Practice:
God, thank You for the discovery process. I rejoice in knowing that You have no desire to keep things that You have in mind for me concealed and hidden forever. I submit to Your perfect revelations and Your perfect timing and declare that You are a good God who wants me to know who I am and what

I am to do. I receive my God-purpose in Jesus' name and I declare that You are revealing it to me more and more each day. I declare that as I discover, I define, and as I define, I discover... this is so fun... I receive the adventure of discovering and pursuing my purpose! In Jesus' name I pray, amen.

Enforcing You

Verse:

> *"If you abide in Me, and My words abide in you, you will ask what you desire, and it shall be done for you." John 15:7*

Declaration:

God, I thank You for inviting me to abide in Your presence and to saturate myself with Your nature of love. I declare that I am at home with You and that I earnestly desire to tarry with You every moment of the day. I declare that Your Word lives within me and navigates the passions of my heart. Thank You that as I sit in Your presence, You fulfill the needs and wants of my heart. I am satisfied in every way. I declare a rest in Your presence alone. In Jesus' name I pray, amen.

Self-Reconciliation:

(Insert your name), you are at home in the presence of God. I declare that you abide in His heart every moment of the day. I speak His love poured out within you; you are saturated with His love. The Word of God is in you, and you meditate on it day and night. Every desire of your heart is a passion of God's and you are confident that He will fulfill all that He has put in your heart to do. In Jesus' name, let it be done! Amen.

Chapter Seven
Setting and Accomplishing Goals

As a culture, we have bought in to the importance of goal setting as a key component to success. However, too many of us fail to accomplish our goals. We set goals with much enthusiasm and excitement, and we shoot out of the gates with every intention to "get 'er done" but many more goals remain *undone* than *get done*.

One of the top trending hashtags every January is #resolutionfail. While approximately 45% of people set New Year's resolutions, only 8% follow through. Fitness clubs literally bank on resolution failures each year. Most fitness club owners admit that they oversell their yearly membership capacity at the start of every year, knowing that over half won't last more than two weeks. They capitalize on the public's inability to follow through and accomplish goals. We must not only learn to set goals, we must learn to follow through and accomplish them.

SETTING GOALS

"Suppose one of you wants to build a tower. Won't you first sit down and estimate the cost to see if you have enough money to complete it? For if you lay the foundation and are not able to

finish it, everyone who sees it will ridicule you,
saying, 'This person began to build and wasn't
able to finish." Luke 14:28

The Bible is very clear that setting goals is a key component to finishing what you set out to do. Much like a New Year's resolution, it is too easy to say you *want* to do something and never actually do it. I like to say there are many who have faith, but few who are faithful. Our spirit is willing, but the flesh is weak (see Matthew 26:41), so without a plan, we will likely fail. Many of us have great intentions, but until we are intentional, they will never come to pass. This is what goal setting is all about. It is choosing to be intentional about accomplishing what is in your heart. It is more than just talking about it.

> *"For a dream comes through much activity,*
> *And a fool's voice is known by his many words.*
> *When you make a vow to God, do not delay to*
> *pay it;*
> *For He has no pleasure in fools.*
> *Pay what you have vowed—*
> *Better not to vow than to vow and not pay."*
> *Ecclesiastes 5:3-5*

We know that our dreams will require action on our part. This is the "much activity" referred to in Ecclesiastes. I like to call it partnering with God. He gives you a vision, and your goals are the necessary actions that activate that vision. Anybody can talk about a dream; it is the voice of a fool that just speaks about it but never moves on it. God says that when you decide you want to pursue your dream, you better be serious about what you say. Don't throw your ideas and dreams around carelessly. Be intentional to follow through on what you are speaking. Responding to your purpose is like going into a business venture with God, and you need to be prepared to pay what you have vowed. In other words, follow through on your part! Don't sit back and do nothing, victimized by happenstance that never "happens" to you. Every place where God speaks a word to His people, there is an invitation to add action to the word. Do you want to be healed? Go and wash, stretch out your hand, take up your mat, go and present yourselves! These actions, DONE IN FAITH, were the "much activity" that released the promise in their lives. God's word PLUS your action is what equals the promise. Partnership! If you don't plan on participating in the mani-festation of your purpose, then don't talk about it!

WISE GOALS

There is more to it than just setting goals, we must learn HOW to set goals. Too often we don't accomplish our goals because they are simply not the "right" goals, or wise goals. Wise goals are personalized to YOU as well as to the season you are in. This is why our housing program designed the Individual Spiritual Plan (ISP) for our residents. It is what we use to set goals with each resident based on who they are, where they are headed, and what season they are in. We remind them continuously that their program looks different from other residents because their program is individualized. We remind them that setting a goal based on what everyone else is doing is setting them up to fail. We should keep this in mind for ourselves as well. I think twice before I raise my hand to jump in on a "community goal." Just because everyone else is doing it does not mean you *have to* or even *should*. The first step in goal setting is making sure the goals are relevant to YOU. I like to set goals that are God-given, purpose-driven, and slightly uncomfortable!

GOD-GIVEN

> *"May He grant you according to your heart's desire,*
> *And fulfill all your purpose." Psalm 20:4*

The word purpose here in Hebrew implies the idea of having a plan. I like to say that goal setting is your plan of action. It is the road map to start the journey of moving toward your destiny.

Read Psalm 20:4 in The Voice translation:

> *"May He grant the dreams of your heart*
> *and see your plans through to the end."*

God wants to "see us through our plans"

because He knows that having plans are the key to fulfilling your dreams; plans bring about an end result. Simply said, He is in favor of having a plan. More specifically, a God-driven plan says, "I am partnering with God in the fulfillment of my purpose." It is important that we understand that our goals are set to partner with God in what He has set out to do through us. It is NOT the reverse. We should not set goals and then ask God to partner with us. A key to accomplishing goals is setting the goals God has in mind for you. Your goals are simply to get you caught up to where God sees you in the Spirit; they are to move you into your purpose. Remember, He already knows your tomorrow. Isaiah 46:10 declares that God knows "the end from the beginning."

God is already IN your tomorrow, and He is beckoning you forward. This is what a shepherd does; he leads from the front and guides his sheep. Keep your eye on Him and allow Him to impress the goals that need to be set for you. He has had your "end" in sight from the very beginning. Since He knows where you are going, it makes sense that you let Him design your plan of action.

PURPOSE-DRIVEN

Goals are the building blocks to your purpose; they are the steppingstones to your dreams. Therefore, your purpose should decide your goals for you. Speaking of "seeing the end from the beginning," there is a worksheet included at the end of the book about writing a one-year narrative. It inspires you to consider what your life looks like in one year and write it out in narrative form. After you write the narrative, think about what must happen in order to accomplish that narrative. The reason for the exercise is to allow the big picture of your tomorrow to decide the "small steps" of your today. Defining the things that have to happen helps to identify goals that are relevant to getting you there. Often, we don't accomplish our goals simply because they are not relevant to where we want to be. In other words, they are not connected to our purpose; they are not purpose-driven.

One of the biggest things I focus on as a life coach is not just goal setting but setting purpose-driven goals. Remember, if you aren't accomplishing your goals, it could simply be that you are setting the wrong goals. This chapter on goal setting is a practical part of enforcing your purpose, but the chapters that precede it are keys to accomplishing those goals. Our goals *must* be rooted in our purpose or we will indeed fail. This goes back to the concept of intrinsic motivation and how we feel internally motivated to do what is close to our hearts. Your purpose must be the "why" behind your goals.

No one wants to do a puzzle without seeing the picture, the outcome. The picture on the box shows what we are aiming for. We use the picture to help us decide what piece to pick up next and where to place it. We refer to the picture frequently because it navigates us to the fulfillment of the puzzle. It is the end that we get to see while we are still at the beginning. Likewise, our purpose helps to decide what goals we should set and why. This is why we write our vision down; it is the big picture on the box that we need to continually refer to. It is the end that we see, even while we are still at the beginning.

UNCOMFORTABLE GOALS

Another key to setting "the right" goals is to set goals that will stretch you and challenge you. We already established that your purpose is bigger than you can imagine, so our goals should also be "bigger" than us. We should recognize that God uses our goals to teach us and train us how to stay out of the comfort zones of life. Isn't it true that the whole point to setting goals is to establish new habits and enforce a change in our lives? God uses them to push us beyond the familiar and the comfortable and into the next "level" of capacity. This is a vital part of God's training that prepares you for your purpose. If we set goals that are in our comfort zones, we will never grow. Your comfort zone will become the determining factor of your capacity. Instead, goals should be set to *intentionally* increase capacity so that ultimately you are better prepared to bear the "bigness" of your purpose.

I have heard it said that there are comfort goals, discomfort goals, and delusional goals. They say that you should aim for discomfort goals, or goals that are outside of your comfort level. But I think that the Holy Spirit always adds an element of delusional in there as well. As a life coach, I tell my clients to think somewhere between discomfort and delusional when they are setting their goals. While we do want to set goals that are "doable," we also want to set ourselves up to depend on God and His power. Setting slightly delusional goals will force you to rely on God; it puts a demand on His hand to work in you and through you to accomplish what would be impossible (or just temporary) in your flesh. This is how you stretch your capacity from the natural to the supernatural. When fulfilling my purpose, I want to put a demand on God's hand in it—so I MUST set goals slightly outside of what I can perceive.

While there are many acronyms out there to help you set good goals, none of them will matter if they are not God-given and purpose-driven. This is why all the previous chapters were so imperative to get through before jumping into this content. Many of us have heard of SMART goals, which I fully believe in, but the smartest goals are the ones that will usher you into your dreams. See the worksheet called "The Goal Connection" at the back of this book.

ACCOMPLISHING GOALS

We have discussed the importance of the kinds of goals that you set; they are a key component to setting yourself up for success in accomplishing them. But let's talk more specifically about things that you should do to ensure follow through on your goals.

WRITING YOUR GOALS

Many people set goals in their heads but don't take the time to write them down. Research shows that you are 42 percent more likely to achieve your goals if you write them down. There are many reasons given for this, but I believe it is because of the visual aspect of seeing them. Writing them down helps to clearly define the tasks necessary to move you forward in your purpose. You may *think* you know what you need to do in your head, but you might be surprised by how unclear it is once you capture it on paper. I HIGHLY recommend using goal sheets of some sort to help navigate you to specific and measurable goals (SMART goals).

I also encourage my clients to describe their goals. It is also proven that vividly describing your goals will better set you up for success. This is because the imagination is activated through the process. The more you can visualize yourself doing the goal, the more likely you are to accomplish the goal. In some regard, the goal must become a part of who you are since it is a building block to your purpose.

> *"By faith he dwelt in the land of promise as in a foreign country, dwelling in tents with Isaac and Jacob, the heirs with him of the same promise..." Hebrews 11:9*

This verse recently jumped out at me because of the phrase, "he dwelt in the land of promise." I felt the Holy Spirit prompt me to consider what it looks like to "dwell in the land of promise." Abraham died never receiving his promise, yet this verse says he dwelt there. This is mind blowing! I believe the Holy Spirit was encouraging me to dwell in my promise, mentally, emotionally, and spiritually. He wants me to think about it, imagine it, dream about it, and talk about it. He wants us to act as though it is even though it might not yet be (see Romans 4:17). The more we can activate this through the goal setting process, the better!

CONNECT WITH YOUR GOALS

> *"Jesus said to him, 'You shall love the LORD your God with all your heart, with all your soul, and with all your mind.'" Matthew 22:37*

I believe this verse reminds us of what "full engagement" looks like in anything we do. God wants us to be all-in—body, soul, and spirit. In Luke, this verse includes loving God "with all your strength" as well, which supports the idea of physical activity or action. So what does this have to do with goals? I have found that connecting with our goals spiritually, intellectually, emotionally, as well as physically helps ensure the success of completing them. We know that accomplishing our goals will require physical work in that we must add action to the goal, or it will never get done. But what does it mean to connect with them spiritually, intellectually, and emotionally?

INTELLECTUAL CONNECTION

Connecting intellectually is what I like to call "the mind connection." Connecting intellectually tends to be the easiest for us, and frankly, most people automatically do it. It simply means setting goals that "make sense" in our minds, or intellectually. However, I like to take it a step further and try to connect intellectually on the other end of the goal, once the goal is completed. This can be done by asking, "Where do you see yourself once this goal is accomplished?" Or, "Why is this goal necessary to tomorrow?" Or, "How is this goal pertinent to your purpose?" These are just some of the questions you can ask yourself. The idea is to see yourself on the other side of the goal from the perspective that it is already done. This goes back to visualizing who you will be BEFORE you get there. It gives you the end goal from the beginning, which is how we start the intrinsic motivation process. That visual is the finish line that keeps you focused and running all the way through.

SPIRITUAL CONNECTION

Connecting spiritually to a goal is simply being convinced it is a God-given, purpose-driven goal. You want to be intentional about this process. Instead of just knowing it, you can make self-declarations like, "My spirit bears witness with the importance of this goal." Or, "I am confident that this goal is necessary in preparing me for the fulfillment of my purpose." Making such statements will keep you connected spiritually and will fan the flame of your purpose. You also want to connect spiritually on the other side of the goal. Here are some good questions to ask yourself: "How do I expect God to mature me spiritually through this goal?" Or, "Who will I be once this goal is completed?"

Finally, we connect with our goals spiritually by praying about them and for them. Talk to God about your goals and ask Him to continually give you the energy and desire to see them through. Philippians 2:13 says: "it is God who works in you both to will and to do for His good pleasure." The word "works" in Greek is the word "energeo." It means "to be operative or put forth power." It is where we get the English word "energy," which I think best helps grasp what is being said. It is only by the inner working of the Holy Spirit that you are stirred or energized to fulfill your God-given goals. He empowers you to get it done. You must claim that as a promise when you are growing weary in the midst of fulfilling your goals. If it is God-ordained and purpose-driven, then there is enough energy to see it through. Draw on that energy by talking to God about your goals and staying connected to them spiritually.

EMOTIONAL CONNECTION

Your purpose starts in the heart, and because you are passionate about something, you begin to move towards that purpose by setting goals. The problem is we quickly shift from our heart to our head when we do this, UNLESS we are intentional to connect with the goals emotionally. So, we know where our goals will take us and what it will look like when a goal is accomplished, but how will you *feel* once it is completed? Without the heart, we will lose passion, and without passion, we will lose unction, which drives our intrinsic motivation. So, when setting a goal ask yourself questions like, "How do I feel about this goal?" Or, "How will I feel when I am working on this goal?"

We want to connect to the other side of this goal emotionally as well. "How will I feel once I have accomplished this goal?" This may seem silly, but we are more driven by the heart than we are by the mind. God designed us to be motivated that way. By connecting emotionally, you fuel yourself with passion and energy to see the goal all the way through.

CONNECT DAILY

Read your goals daily. Post them around your spaces, record yourself talking about them, and listen to yourself speak them while you are driving. Remember, we want to dwell IN the promise. As much as you can, write down statements that declare your connections and read them OUT LOUD daily. This might look like...

- I declare that this goal is necessary to move me closer to my purpose.
- I declare that when I accomplish this goal, I will be delighted in my progress.
- I declare that this goal is easy because it is prompted by the Holy Spirit.
- I declare that when I accomplish this goal, I will feel free.
- I declare that this goal fits who I am and where I am heading.

Write your own words as well, and intentionally cultivate your connections to your goals because they are the building blocks to your dreams.

IDENTIFYING BARRIERS AND CORE LIES

I often ask clients once they have set their goals to identify what might keep them from accomplishing their goals. In other words, what are the potential dangers or threats to your goals? By identifying these ahead of time, you can decide in advance how you plan to overcome those barriers. There is power in predetermination. It removes any emotional decisions or choices that need to be made "on the fly," because the decision has already been made. This exercise of predetermining is powerful in many aspects of life. Determine ahead of time who you want to be when you talk to THAT person, when you face THAT trial, when you have THAT conversation, when you face THAT temptation. And then visualize yourself overcoming that barrier. Again, mentally exercise who you want to be and who you are designed to be.

Identifying barriers also helps to identify core lies. A barrier for me is "interruptions." This is also what we call a "tolerance" (see the "What are your Tolerances?" worksheet). I have a tendency to lack boundaries that keep me from being interrupted when I am in the middle of something important to me. This drives me to ask, "Why?" For me, the answer is that I don't want to be inaccessible or unavailable to those around me. But let's take this a step further to identify a core lie behind this. Using myself as an example, in this case, the core lie is that what I am doing is not as important as what everyone else needs. Let's take it a step further. Core lie: My purpose is not as valuable as everyone else's. THERE IT IS! You're welcome for the vulnerable confession.

We can also identify core lies when a goal has been set for several weeks but has been left undone. Don't get discouraged and quit. Ask yourself why. If you are confident that it is a God-given, purpose-driven goal, then what is your hang up? This is not a failure; it is an opportunity to grow and allow the Lord to refine your heart.

I recently asked a client why he thinks he continuously falls short of his goals. He responded, and I quote, "Because I am a procrastinator." Is this really who you are or is it something that you struggle with? The first thing I had to do was separate his struggle from his identity. This is where Enforcing YOU and who you are designed to be is GREATLY important and applicable to helping you accomplish your goals. You can't be both a child of God who is designed in the image of God AND be a procrastinator. God is an on-time God and He has designed us to flow in HIS perfect timing. In the Spirit, we live "for such a time as this." Again, if your goals are God-given, then we know the timing is NOW. Don't allow character flaws and bad habits to become your identity! Identifying his barrier of procrastination revealed more than just a barrier, it revealed a core lie. The pattern of procrastination caused me to ask, "Why?" In this case the answer was, "I am afraid to try and fail so I just continue to put it off." Core lie: I fear failure. More poignantly: My value is directly connected to my success.

This process was expounded on in my book *Enforcing YOU*. If you can, refer back to chapter six and read it through the lens of identifying barriers that keep you from accomplishing your goals. It is important that you don't ignore your barriers. They will tell you something about you! Press into that with the Holy Spirit and let Him heal you and set you up to accomplish all you put your hand to! This is what it means to "lay aside every weight, and the sin which so easily ensnares us" (see Heb. 12:1) so that we can run our race without any deeply rooted lies holding us back! You and I are designed to prosper; this means we are set up for success in regard to accomplishing our goals. If you feel that you are experiencing anything less, you might want to consider your core lies as anchors keeping you from sailing ahead.

FREEDOM GOALS

I think it is important to remember that goals are to set you free, not to enslave you. Much like we do on the Word of God, we should stay focused on the spirit of the goal, meaning the purpose behind it. Sometimes we don't accomplish the letter of the goal or exactly what we wrote down, yet we still moved forward in regard to the purpose of the goal. This should be celebrated! Don't allow goals to shame you, allow progress to motivate you and remind you of your purpose.

We are to navigate our goals and not be navigated BY our goals. They should not control you, nor should you be obsessive about them. When you feel that you are bogged down or burdened by goals, you can be sure that they are not God-given, but rather flesh-driven. Many people are "naturally driven" and want to accomplish MORE than what God is asking within that season (I resemble that remark). There will be no spiritual "help" in those kinds of goals because you will be functioning solely out of your own flesh. You can be sure that they will drain you and discourage you. More goals are not better, GOD goals are! If and when you feel captivated by your goals, go back to

God and ask what He wants for you in THIS season. While God does want to challenge and stretch you through your goals, He does NOT want to crush you.

Goals are also meant to free you because once they are accomplished, they signify that you are done! Some people need goals as parameters or boundaries to STOP working and rest. When God created the world, there was a sense of satisfaction in His work, then He rested!

> *"Then God saw everything that He had made, and indeed it was very good. So the evening and the morning were the sixth day. Thus the heavens and the earth, and all the host of them, were finished. And on the seventh day God ended His work which He had done, and He rested on the seventh day from all His work which He had done. Then God blessed the seventh day and sanctified it, because in it He rested from all His work which God had created and made." Genesis 1:31-2:3*

While goals are a great way to ensure what we need to be doing, they are also a great way to ensure when we need to STOP doing. They will free you from overworking and never resting.

SUCCESS METERS

Everyone wants to be successful. More so, we want to FEEL successful. So we look for ways to define and measure success. This can be discouraging if you look through the eyes of the world. The world will tell us that success is all about outcome and results, but success in the Kingdom is all about who we are becoming on the inside.

When I first started the housing program at Crazy8 Ministries, I prayed that 100% of the residents who came in would leave completely set free and restored from poverty. I wanted it to be perfect! After about six months, we had our first "issues" with a resident. Simply put, she needed to be removed from the program. I grieved through this; I mean, I literally ached at the thought. The act of removing someone was completely counter-intuitive to the whole purpose of the mission, and my heart was so broken. I struggled deeply with feeling like a failure and wrestled with "what might be wrong with the program." I wanted it to be so perfect that everyone would feel the love of Jesus and succeed.

This was the point in my life where God taught me how to measure success. Specifically, He reminded me that He Himself had died for ALL; that He was "not willing that any should perish." He reminded me that His only purpose was to die so that all might live through and in Him. He then whispered in my ear, "Though I gave 100%, even I am not getting a 100% return." WOW! That was pivotal. The success of Jesus wasn't based on the return; it was based on His obedience to the plan. And His plan literally IS perfect. I learned through this that success is not about results and it is not about perfection.

First and foremost, let your obedience be a success meter. If you are obedient to Him, no matter the outcome, you are successful. Be confident in that. Don't let what you see around you measure you. Don't confuse outcome with obedience. God is more concerned with your heart than He is your circumstance; He will prioritize working inside of you before He works on the outside. This can be difficult because our flesh wants to SEE evidence of our labors. If you only allow what you see to affirm you, you will experience discouragement as you move forward in your goals. Remember, we want to stay focused on the spirit of the goal, not the letter of the goal. God is ALWAYS at work, and He is ALWAYS doing something. Stay focused on what He has told you to do. Be tenacious and stubborn in obedience and allow the reward of walking in the pleasure of your King to be your measure of success.

Let progress be a success meter. Perfection is a deceitful concept that will keep you always striving but never arriving. Simply put, perfection should not be a measure of success. I heard it once said that you should always measure your success by your yesterday. I love this because while setting goals helps to "measure" our forward movement, they should not be our measure of success. Goals measure progress, not success. Hear me, we should not be striving for perfection; we should strive for progress. Even Paul said that it wasn't about perfection, but rather about moving forward.

"Not that I have already attained, or am already perfected; but I press on, that I may lay hold of that for which Christ Jesus has also laid hold of me." Philippians 3:12

Paul realized that walking with God isn't about being perfect; it is about moving forward DESPITE OUR IMPERFECTION. That is the whole point of grace. God has given us a forward lean in life through the Holy Spirit. He will cause you to progress because you are designed to prosper. Let your forward progression be the measure. You might not SEE progress; instead, you might just feel progress. Isn't this what we really want anyway? We all know someone who is successful from a worldly perspective, yet they don't FEEL successful. This is why God Himself must be your voice of standard. Look to Him to measure your success from the inside, not the outside.

Goals are important, but you must be intentional to invite God to sit with you as you consider the goals that are necessary to begin moving forward. Let the Holy Spirit reveal God-given and purpose-driven goals and let Him motivate you to accomplish them. He is perfect in all of His ways (see Proverbs 18:30) and He knows your end from the beginning (see Isaiah 46:10). He will not fail you, mislead you, nor abandon you.

Trust Him to reveal the building blocks necessary to bring you into your promised land. God Himself will empower you to enforce your purpose through every goal.

Prayer Practice:

God, I am overwhelmed with how lovingly interested you are in every detail of my life. You care about every aspect and are in every moment of my forward movement. I declare that YOU are my "Goal setter." YOU are the "Building Block," and YOU are the "Steppingstone" that navigates me into my purpose. You are not a God who teases me, but You put in me all that You have in mind for me. Thank You for giving me goals that are driven by my purpose You put within me! I am honored to heed the call. I press onward and upward to my heavenly assignment. In Jesus' name I pray, amen.

Enforcing You

Verse:

> *"May He grant you according to your heart's desire,*
> *And fulfill all your purpose." Psalm 20:4*

> *"May God give you every desire of your heart and carry out your every plan as you go to battle." The Passion translation*

*"May he give you the desire of your heart
and make all your plans succeed." NIV*

Declaration:

*I declare that according to all You have put in
my heart, I am granted Your favor. I speak a
Kingdom movement over every goal and over every
plan as I move forward in the passions of my heart.
Thank You, God, that You cause my plans to succeed
and You establish the work of my hands according to
Your purpose and my calling.*

Self-Reconciliation:

*(Insert name here), God desires to grant you
the desires of your heart. His hand is on you and your
purpose. He wants you to move forward and has put
it in you to do the "work" to see it through. You are
designed to succeed in the Kingdom and as you obey
His heart, He will cause you to flourish in your
purpose. Rest in Him.*

Chapter Eight
Persevering in the Waiting

As I was just starting out building Crazy8 Ministries, I asked a mentor of mine what she felt was the most important character trait in fulfilling your purpose. Without any hesitation she answered, "Perseverance." Honestly, I was shocked. I thought she would say something like wisdom, or joy... or love! Perseverance? Why perseverance? She told me that over the years she had watched many people start out pursuing their dreams with great energy and passion, but they ended up growing weary and quitting. They had vision, they had a plan, and they had a purpose, but they lacked perseverance. Anybody can start something; the true test of character is: Will you see it through?

> *"And let us not grow weary while doing good, for in due season we shall reap if we do not lose heart." Galatians 6:9*

There is a promise of a harvest time in this verse. But I don't think we like that little phrase, "in due season." What in the world does that even mean? Let's face it, we want our harvest yesterday and we want it to come easily. We don't like to wait, and we don't like to struggle. In reality, though, fulfilling your purpose will never come as quickly as you want it to, and it will never be as "easy" as you want it to be. God put this verse in the Bible for a reason. He knew man's inclination is to grow weary, in other words, to give up. He addresses this to encourage the character of perseverance. I cannot tell you how many times I have gone through seasons where I have literally repeated to myself OUT LOUD, "For in due season I SHALL reap if I faint not" (KJV). Over and over again I have encouraged myself using God's words not to give up and to press on. When I was looking for land for our ministry and was under the gun for time and money, my assistant asked me what she could do to help me. I looked her straight in the face and said, "Your biggest job right now is to never let me give up." She took that very seriously and when we found land, she made me a sign that is still in my office today that says, "Never give up!" I needed that voice, and I needed that encouragement.

Pressing forward toward our purpose will bring great battles. From distractions, to money constraints, to illnesses, to scheduling issues, to fear—you name it, it will happen. Hear me when I say the enemy HATES your purpose. He will do anything to keep you from building your dreams. Remember, he wants to see you shrivel in feelings of insignificance, with no hope of ever having any purpose.

In the book of Ezra, King Cyrus, a Pagan king, was stirred by the Lord to send the Israelites back to Judah to build a temple for the Lord after sixty years of captivity. By grace, their freedom was given to them, but it was given to them for a purpose: to build. Well, in chapters one, two, and three they begin building and get the foundation and the altar restored. Then in chapter four, they meet opposition. The Bible says that adversaries tried to befriend them, but they stayed persistent. When the adversaries didn't work, the Bible then says that their adversaries "hired counselors against them to frustrate their purpose." I am not making this up... check it out...

> "Then the people of the land tried to discourage the people of Judah. They troubled them in building, and hired counselors against them to frustrate their purpose all the days of Cyrus king of Persia, even until the reign of Darius king of Persia." Ezra 4:4&5

Friends, I am here to tell you that the enemy hasn't changed. He doesn't come up with new tricks. He is a liar who will send anything or anyone to frustrate your purpose. The people of God would not compromise their building by "making friends with their adversary," so their adversary sent "frustrations." The word discourage in this verse means "to weaken the hands," and the word frustrate means "to break or make ineffectual." Doesn't this adequately describe what happens to us as we are trying to build our dreams? We get frustrated with the multitude of "things," and we grow weary and fainthearted. One of the saddest verses in Scripture is Ezra 4:24.

> *"Thus the work of the house of God which is at Jerusalem ceased, and it was discontinued until the second year of the reign of Darius king of Persia."*

An inability to persevere will bring your dreams to a halt. The definition of perseverance is "continued effort to do or achieve something despite difficulties, failure, or opposition." Read that definition a few times and tell me that isn't a difficult thing to do! I don't care who you are, persevering is hard, but if you are going to succeed, you must determine now that you will continue in your efforts despite difficulties, failure, or opposition. Decide now! Don't wait till you are in the heat of your emotions and battles or you will fail. Remember, everyone has a dream, but not everyone will see it through. Decide today that YOU WILL!

WAITING

Waiting can be one of the most frustrating things when you are passionate about your purpose and it can certainly lead to giving you a faint heart. Isaiah talks about the importance of waiting when facing weariness and faintheartedness in Isaiah 40.

"Even the youths shall faint and be weary,
And the young men shall utterly fall,
But those who wait on the LORD
Shall renew their strength;
They shall mount up with wings like eagles,
They shall run and not be weary,
They shall walk and not faint."
Isaiah 40:30&31

You don't want to miss the promise given in these verses. Isaiah gives an antidote to weariness. **Wait.** In fact, he said that waiting will bring about strength, which is the opposite of feeling faint. This "advice" sounds a bit like an oxymoron and almost a little like a joke. I know that when I am feeling anxious and faint about when my purpose will come to pass, the last thing I want to hear is the advice "to wait." How is it that waiting can renew us in times of weariness? The answer is found in the definition of waiting. The Hebrew word for wait means "to look for, to hope, and to expect." It actually implies the idea of binding together or twisting. To wait upon the Lord means that we are eagerly looking toward Him to the point of pressing in and getting all twisted up in Him. It means that we are working toward being bound together with Him. This is not inactivity; it shows waiting is an action. So what does this look like? What should we actively and intentionally be doing during the waiting?

STAY PASSIONATE

It is important that we don't lose our passion when we are in seasons of waiting. Paul told Timothy to intentionally fan the flames of his gifts. This is an excellent way to stay passionate.

> *"Therefore I remind you to stir up the gift of God which is in you through the laying on of my hands." 1 Timothy 1:6*

Using your gifts whenever you can will remind you of the call that is on your life as well as keep you excited and passionate. There is nothing worse than feeling like our gifts are no longer available, or that we have lost them. The gifts of God are without repentance (see Romans 11:29). This means God doesn't change His mind and take them back. They are irrevocable. However, not using your gifts will cause you to feel like they are. Whenever and however you can, use your gifts. I love to preach and speak. I don't always have "gigs" or events, but I will still write messages and speak them however I can. Whoever will listen, I always have something to say. That is one of the reasons why I write books. God has put it in my heart to preach His Truth and writing is one of my outlets for communicating to others.

We also stay passionate by "dwelling on the promise." Hebrews 11:9 tells us that Abraham "dwelt in the land of promise" even though he died never having arrived in it. As I'd mentioned, I recently was wrecked by that revelation. What does it mean to dwell in something that hasn't yet come to fruition? Consider that question spiritually, mentally, and emotionally. Consider it in the words we speak, in the conversations we have, and in the company we keep. I believe that is absolutely imperative to be obnoxiously focused on your purpose. Now, try not to be obnoxiously annoying to your friends, but you should have friends who love to hear about your dreams and aspirations. You should have friends with whom conversations about passions are normal and encouraged.

> *"Let us consider one another in order to stir up love and good works, not forsaking the assembling of ourselves together, as is the manner of some, but exhorting one another..."*
> *Hebrews 10:24&25*

Be sure that your tight circle looks like this. It may only be one or two people, and that's OK. But don't compromise your dreams just to have more friends. Negativity and nay-sayers will ultimately crush your spirit and shatter your dreams.

Most importantly, you should be having these conversations with God and with yourself. Dream-build with God and let the Holy Spirit take you to your dreams in your mind. Remember the power of your imagination. Emotionally live as if your purpose is established because in the Spirit, it is! Set your mind on the excellence of His purpose for your life and refuse to think about anything less.

LEAN FORWARD

Keep a posture of leaning forward as you wait. This is done by setting goals and always doing the next "thing." As you stay connected and bound to God, He will give you ways to keep your posture tipped toward the finish line. This is also to be done in the mind and heart. You must remain confident in God and His promise!

> *"Therefore do not cast away your confidence, which has great reward. For you have need of endurance, so that after you have done the will of God, you may receive the promise...*
> *'Now the just shall live by faith;*
> *But if anyone draws back,*
> *My soul has no pleasure in him.'*
> *But we are not of those who draw back to perdition, but of those who believe to the saving of the soul." Hebrews 10:35-39*

Confidence means I will not shrink back, I will not hesitate, and I will not cower. Too many times we accept the idea of hesitancy as being cautious or using wisdom, but I fear it typically is nothing more than losing our forward lean in Christ. It is easy to be confident when we are sure. It is more challenging to be confident when we aren't sure. Assuredness too often wanes, but our confidence must not. It is possible to remain confident even when we are not sure. This is because our confidence is in God. In Him I am sure even when I am unsure of anything else. I often say, "I can know nothing, but I know God and therefore, I know everything." I may not know what or where or how or when, but I know the One who does. He is the reason why I am leaning forward. We must refuse to lean back except to rest on His chest. His heartbeat is where we find our confidence and thus the strength to endure.

> *"Let us draw near with a true heart in full assurance of faith, having our hearts sprinkled from an evil conscience and our bodies washed with pure water. Let us hold fast the confession of our hope without wavering, for He who promised is faithful." Hebrews 10:22&23*

Let His presence keep you anchored in His promises. Remember He is not a man that He should lie (see Numbers 23:19). He does not repent from His Word and He does not change His mind. He means what He says, and He says what He means. Be intentional to listen to Him and let His whisper tip you into a forward lean as you wait.

STAY READY

Staying "ready" is important in times of waiting. This means preparing YOU. As a counselor, the best thing I can do to prepare for a day when I am meeting with 6-8 clients back to back is prepare

ME. This is true of anything we are doing. I can write a really great message, but if my heart is not right with God, it will have no anointing on it. When you are waiting, to the same degree that you are pursuing God, you must be preparing you. This is the whole reason why I included the Enforcing YOU sections in this book. Hear me when I say that we should NEVER pursue our purpose more than we pursue our personal design. Too many times we see people lose themselves to their dreams. They sacrifice their health, their families, their ideas, their values, and eventually their own design in Christ. This is why it is so important to guard your heart, ABOVE ALL ELSE (recall Proverbs 24:3). Everything you do flows out from your heart, so if your heart is broken, sick, or compromised, your life will be, too.

It is one thing to be ready, it is another to STAY ready. This requires a continuum of working out your salvation (see Philippians 2:12) and cultivating your design in Christ. Remember, your gifts will get you there, and character will keep you there. While this whole book has been about "getting to" your purpose, know there is purpose in your today. Conversely, just because where you are today has purpose, this does not mean it is your final destiny. Don't confuse waiting with laziness or apathy. God never wastes a day. He uses every moment of your life to prepare you for tomorrow. Even the leftovers were collected after Jesus fed the multitude in Matthew 14. We learn that nothing in the Kingdom is ever wasted. God gathers up the rubble of our lives and uses it to build us into our fullest potential and fulfill our purpose.

Stay ready and girded up so that you can stand in the battles of fear, discouragement, disappointment, trials, failures, and betrayals. Ephesians 6 reminds us that we must put on the armor of God so that "having done all" we can stand!

> *"Therefore take up the whole armor of God, that you may be able to withstand in the evil day, and having done all, to stand. Stand therefore, having girded your waist with truth, having put on the breastplate of righteousness, and having shod your feet with the preparation of the gospel of peace; above all, taking the shield of faith with which you will be able to quench all the fiery darts of the wicked one. And take the helmet of salvation, and the sword of the Spirit, which is the word of God; praying always with all prayer and supplication in the Spirit, being watchful to this end with all perseverance and supplication for all the saints." Ephesians 6:13-18*

These verses are filled with action. They are active things to do while we are waiting; things to prepare ourselves for battle. We persevere by not slacking in these things. See it all the way through to the end... till the deliverance into our purpose.

"The horse is prepared for the day of battle,
But deliverance is of the LORD." Proverbs 31:21

Ultimately the victory is only of the Lord, but in the waiting, we must "make ready our horse." This process not only grows you into your anointing, it also keeps you in a state of readiness in season and out of season.

PRACTICE THANKFULNESS

While you are waiting, it is important that you practice thankfulness. Notice that once again, this is an action. There is a difference between being thankful and practicing thankfulness. Practicing thankfulness means I am going to talk about it. God is always at work and we need to learn to recognize and acknowledge His presence in our lives.

"In all your ways acknowledge Him,
And He shall direct your paths." Proverbs 3:6

The word "acknowledge" in Hebrew denotes the idea of being able to discern. It is more than just verbally acknowledging God, it is the idea that in my heart I can distinguish His hand and His heart in the midst of wilderness, and that is what I focus on. This is the whole concept behind practicing thankfulness. Our days are designed by the words we speak. When you speak about the Truth of God in your life, despite where you are circumstantially, your life shifts into a spiritual existence that supersedes what you are experiencing.

God LOVES to be talked about. It activates His presence and releases His power in your life. Isn't this what we need when we are working toward our purpose and things seem fruitless? I need to know—correction—I need to FEEL His presence in the midst of what feels like nothing. Practicing thankfulness VERBALLY releases Him to continue working on your behalf to fulfill His purpose in your life.

Consider Jesus in the feeding of the multitude. He was brought two fish and five loaves of bread, which was clearly not enough food. However, the Bible tells us that Jesus "gave thanks" for the provision (see Matthew 14:19). This is an interesting character trait we learn from Jesus. When you don't have enough, what is your first response? Do you thank Him for what you DO have? Are you acknowledging what you DO see before you complain about what you don't see?

In my book *Mastering Your Seasons* I talk about the trap of complaining. The word complain denotes the idea of "encamping" or "placing a stake in the ground." In other words, it is a mindset where you aren't just *not* moving forward, but you have decided, "I would rather hang out here and talk about THIS." The enemy wants to point out your lack, he wants to point out what you DON'T have, and then keep you stuck thinking about it.

In 2 Kings 4, the prophet Elisha met a widow

145

who started her conversation with him by testifying of all the things that were wrong in her life. She essentially expressed that she was focused on all the reasons why she had no hope. The prophet responded with what I think is a brilliant question.

> *"So Elisha said to her, 'What shall I do for you? Tell me, what do you have in the house?'"*
> *2 Kings 4:2*

It is almost as if he dismisses her laundry list of reasons why she has no hope. His question forces her mind to shift from what is NOT to what IS. While we don't want to dismiss her reality, see that God was still at work. She was looking at circumstances and NOT at God. Practicing thankfulness keeps us focused on God and what He is doing and shatters the mirage of our circumstances that would tell us nothing is happening, nothing is working, I don't have enough, it can't be done, or it is impossible. This should not shock us. Jesus said that with man all things are impossible, BUT WITH GOD, all things are possible (see Matthew 19:26). Looking at things through our fleshly perspective, it will absolutely look impossible because without God, it is!

1 Thessalonians 5:18 reminds us to "Give thanks in ALL circumstances." This is not natural, so we must be intentional to practice this attribute. It is our BEST defense against discouragement. We

must learn to practice speaking what IS and stop speaking about what is not! This is the entire premise of Paul's exhortation in Philippians 4.

> *"Rejoice in the Lord always. Again I will say, rejoice!*
>
> *"Let your gentleness be known to all men. The Lord is at hand.*
>
> *"Be anxious for nothing, but in everything by prayer and supplication, with thanksgiving, let your requests be made known to God; and the peace of God, which surpasses all understanding, will guard your hearts and minds through Christ Jesus.*
>
> *"Finally, brethren, whatever things are true, whatever things are noble, whatever things are just, whatever things are pure, whatever things are lovely, whatever things are of good report, if there is any virtue and if there is anything praiseworthy—meditate on these things. The things which you learned and received and heard and saw in me, these do, and the God of peace will be with you." Philippians 4:4-9*

I would be willing to bet that most of you could quote much of that passage, and I would also be willing to bet that most of you are doing what it instructs. So why you are still filled with anxiety, worry, and discouragement? Not only do we leave out the phrase "with thanksgiving," we don't practice meditating on the "God things." The verse says "these do," a profound little clause that changes what is promised.

I remember when I struggled with anxiety and depression years ago and I sat at a table with some women who had also struggled. Many of them had been set free and were sharing what God had told them to do. I was miffed because He had told me the same things, yet I still struggled. I mentioned that to one of the ladies and she lovingly looked me straight in the eyes and said, "But did you DO it?" Essentially, she taught me that knowing WHAT to do isn't what sets you free, DOING it does!

IT WILL COME

We looked intently at Habakkuk 2:2 and the importance of writing down the vision, but verse 3 lets us in on a secret.

> *"For the vision is yet for an appointed time;*
> *But at the end it will speak, and it will not lie.*
> *Though it tarries, wait for it;*
> *Because it will surely come,*
> *It will not tarry."*

Waiting on your vision is inevitable. Your anointing does not necessarily signify the appointing. David waited over twenty years from the time he was anointed to be king to the time he was appointed.

Furthermore, he spent those twenty years serving sheep, his older brothers who mocked him, and a wicked king. Jacob spent twenty years in "the land of Laban," working faithfully yet being deceived, tricked, and misunderstood. Habakkuk 2:3 stresses that there is an appointed time and we must wait for it, even though it tarries for what feels like forever.

Read it in The Voice translation:

"For the vision points ahead to a time I have appointed; it testifies regarding the end, and it will not lie.
Even if there is a delay, wait for it.
It is coming and will come without delay."

Adhere to your vision. Read it, talk about it, practice it, pray about it, and consider it done. Focus on all that God IS doing and resist the urge to complain. Be intentional to practice waiting actively so that you will not lose heart. Guard your heart and cultivate your design. Be passionate about what you want and don't be afraid to talk about it. Keep your eye on the prize and resolve to never give up. Remember, enforcing your purpose hinges on your ability to persevere while you wait!

Prayer Practice:

God, thank You for putting in me a spirit to persevere! I am not designed to shrink back. I am designed to lean forward all the way through to the finish line. I receive Your forward lean in life. I recognize all that You are doing, and I choose to focus on You. I know that not a day of my life is wasted because you are working ALL things together for my good and Your glory. I will wait actively and press into You in every moment. I declare that my purpose is being fulfilled within me! In Jesus' name I pray, amen.

Enforcing You

Verse:

> *"I am the vine, you are the branches. He who abides in Me, and I in him, bears much fruit; for without Me you can do nothing." John 15:5*

> *"If you abide in Me, and My words abide in you, you will ask what you desire, and it shall be done for you." John 15:7*

Declaration:

I declare that You are the vine and I am the branch. As I abide in You, I bear MUCH fruit. I am nothing apart from You, but attached to You, I am fruitful and prosperous. You fill me with desire, Your desire, as I abide in You and everything I ask for aligns with who You are and who You designed me to be. I declare that You are fulfilling the desires of my heart.

Self-Reconciliation:

(Insert your name), you are designed to live off the person of Jesus Christ. You are at home with Him and you remain in Him. Your mind is set on Him and all His ways and therefore your desires are like His. Because you are living off His person, you are fruitful. His character is coming to life in you, and you are fulfilled and satisfied. He is granting you the deepest desires of your heart!

Conclusion

As you move towards fulfilling your purpose, it is important to know that you will never completely arrive. Your purpose is just as much about the journey as it is about the destination. It is a process that keeps you growing. Remember that it is more about what God is doing IN you than it is about what He is doing around you. Therefore, don't seek His hand more than you seek His heart. Moses saw the works of God, but more than anything he wanted to see the glory of God—His character and His person. Moses was not content to practice his purpose without knowing the glory of God (see Exodus 33). He wanted more. Specifically, he wanted to grow more in his intimacy with the person of God. He sought God's heart, not just His hand.

Prosperity is not about what we see, it is about who we are. Your desire to grow and the fruitfulness of your character are more important than gifts. I think Paul sums up beautifully the process of living with purpose in Philippians chapter 3.

> *"Not that I have already attained, or am already perfected; but I press on, that I may lay hold of that for which Christ Jesus has also laid hold of me. Brethren, I do not count myself to have apprehended; but one thing I do, forgetting*

those things which are behind and reaching
forward to those things which are ahead, I press
toward the goal for the prize of the upward call
of God in Christ Jesus." Philippians 3:12-14

Paul knew that life is not about being perfect; it is about pressing on. He knew that leaning forward and keeping your eye on your finish line are the keys to success. You may never know what your purpose looks like played out practically, but you can know the purpose of your design. That is what keeps you moving forward and pursuing your design! Again, this is why the Enforcing YOU sections were so important in this book. They are to keep you focused on who you are!

To be honest, I am still not really sure exactly what the fullness of my purpose looks like. I have glimpses, ideas, thoughts, and most certainly visions written on paper. I have clear goals for each season to take me step-by-step into the next season. However, I am not quite as sure exactly what the fullness of my purpose means. Shocker, right? I used to be freaked out by this and would assume that it meant I didn't know my purpose. But I do! I know what I love, and I know what I don't love. I know where I am passionate, and I know where I am not. I know what makes me tick, and what ticks me off. I know where I am anointed, and I know where I am not. I have learned to groom who I am and trust that it will give way to where I am going. I just follow God one step at a time as I allow the Spirit to daily search and seek me (see Psalm 139).

Remember personal healing, personal discovery, and personal development are vital to your personal deployment (Thank you, Coach Brian Holmes). But not only are they vital to your deployment, they are vital to your sustainment. Again, character is what KEEPS you "there."

Don't assume that just because you don't know exactly what your future looks like that you don't know your purpose. Conversely, don't assume that just because you are sure of your purpose means you know exactly what your future looks like. If that were the case, you would no longer need God.

In Psalm 119, God refers to the Word of God as a lamp that guides you along your path.

> *"Your word is a lamp to my feet*
> *And a light to my path." Psalm 119:105*

The lamp referred to here was an oil lamp that produced a light that was about 3 feet in diameter. That means holding the lamp would illuminate approximately 1.5 feet in front of you, about the length of one step. I am not saying any of this to debunk all that was written in this book, but rather to stress the importance of *who* you are over *where* you are. Again, purpose is more about who you are becoming, not where you are going. This means you will need to live by faith to fulfill your dreams. There are some things you will know, but there will be a lot that you are simply not quite as sure of. That is OK!

Stay focused on God and HIS nature and your design in Christ. He is a good God, and He wants to bless you with your purpose.

BILLY'S GIFT

One of my all-time favorite movie scenes is from *The Polar Express*. In it, the quiet, shy boy, Billy, enters a place where there is a conveyor belt containing piles of gifts. He is not nearly as confident as the other kids, and up until this point in the movie, he has barely spoken. But something happens to Billy when he hears that there is a package from Santa with his name on it. He yells out, "That's me! I'm Billy!" With great excitement he proclaims his identity and therefore connects the gift to himself. He grabs hold of the box with his name on it. He begins to ride the unknown twists and turns of the conveyor belt, not knowing where he would end up, all the while clinging to the box. When he gets to the end, he is "dumped" into a big bag of gifts where he is nearly swallowed up by the weight of all the gifts around him. As he sinks, a tenacity rises in Billy that causes him to cling to the box. His friends begin pulling on one of his hands while with the other, he holds tightly to this box. Here is the best part, Billy finally gets atop the packages and begins to shake the box and says, "I have wanted this my whole life!" But the kicker is that *he hasn't even looked in the box yet.* How does he know that it is what he has wanted his whole life when he doesn't even know what is inside? The answer is because he is confident in the person of Santa and his nature. Billy knows that Santa gets you what you want; he grants your Christmas wish! Billy doesn't need to look inside the box because he knows the heart of Santa. Furthermore, there was also a tag on the box that said, "Don't open till Christmas." Oh, gosh! This only heightens the anticipation of what in the world could be in the box! He must wait! If this doesn't resonate with you, I don't know what will!

Pursue your purpose like Billy pursued that package; hold on to it even when you are not sure of what is "inside the box" or when you will get to open it. Be confident in who you are—your identity in Christ. "That's me! I'm Lisa, God's daughter!" Grab onto your box and be willing to ride the conveyor belt of life; the twists and the turns, even though you don't know what exactly what your gift might be, where it will take you, or when you get to see it come to pass. That's all OK! All you have to be sure of is the person of God and His nature. Cling to him. God wants to grant you the desires of YOUR heart.

"It is what you have wanted your whole life!"

Worksheets

These next pages are filled with some of the worksheets that I have designed, adopted, or adapted over the years of life coaching and counseling. I tried to include ones that are pertinent to things discussed in this book. Please do not dismiss them! You may think you know, but there is something about the exercise of writing and thinking things out. It is how our brains are designed to process. Then, when you include the Word and God and the Holy Spirit into the mix, you cultivate an atmosphere of Divine revelations.

These worksheets will loosen the mind of Christ in you and will give you direction as you move forward toward your purpose, both inside and outside. I pray that you take them seriously and engage with each one of them. You might want to write your answers in a journal so you can come back to these worksheets frequently. I do most of these at the beginning of each year, and I always get something out of working through them.

Breaking Up With Lies

"For the weapons of our warfare are not carnal but mighty in God for pulling down strongholds, casting down arguments and every high thing that exalts itself against the knowledge of God, bringing every thought into captivity to the obedience of Christ." 2 Corinthians 10:4&5

Core lies root themselves deeply within the heart and mind. In some regard, we develop a soul-tie with them, as if they are a person that we have become comfortable with.

1. Take a moment to define an emotion that you struggle with frequently. (Example: anxiety/fear)

EMOTION _____

2. If that emotion were to speak to you, what message would it be sending? (Example: "You need to do well (get it perfect) or you won't be loved")

MESSAGE :

3. Write a "Dear John" letter breaking up with that lie! Personify the lie as if it were a person (it IS indeed a spirit). Write a letter letting that lie know you no longer want to be in covenant with it. Be sure to include all the dangling messages and emotions that stem FROM that one lie!

4. Typically we FEEL emotions physically somewhere in our body. For example: anger in my head, anxiety in my chest, etc. Once you have written your letter, be intentional to "remove" any physical effects that lie has had on you. To do this, simply touch that part of your body and say something like:

"In Jesus' name, I am removing you (fear, anxiety, anger...) from my (chest, head...). We are breaking up and you no longer have any permissions in my body!"

I like to make a motion that is like wiping or pulling something off me (or out of me) and throw it away!

You may need to do this exercise for as many lies you are able to identify.

5. Finally, write a love letter to God recommitting to HIM and HIS Truths. This part is important in that it replaces the former covenant of the lie with a new covenant of Truth.

Differing Opinions of YOU!

"Therefore, from now on, we regard no one according to the flesh…" 2 Corinthians 5:16

"But with me it is a very small thing that I should be judged by you or by a human court. In fact, I do not even judge myself. For I know of nothing against myself, yet I am not justified by this; but He who judges me is the Lord." 1 Corinthians 4:3&4

If your friends were to walk in the room, what would they say about you, or how would they describe you? List three descriptions.

1.

2.

3.

What about your family?

1.

2.

3.

What about YOU? What would you say about yourself, or how would you describe yourself?

1.

2.

3.

What about God?

1.

2.

3.

Which set of descriptions do you identify with the most? To answer this, consider which ones have the most "control" over how you see yourself, or the ones you feel you tend to agree with in your own mind. Also consider why and write down your thoughts.

Which one do you WANT to agree with and want to have the most influence over who you are? Why? In other words, who do you WANT to be? Consider the difference between your reality and what is TRUE.

List some ACTIONS that you can take to start BEING who you want to be.

1.

2.

3.

Identifying the "Things" in your Life

"So do not worry, saying, 'What shall we eat?' or 'What shall
we drink?' or 'What shall we wear?' For the pagans run after
all these things, and your heavenly Father knows that you
need them. But seek first his kingdom and his righteousness,
and all these things will be given to you as well."
Matthew 6:32&33

There are things in our lives that we tend to run to BEFORE
we run to God. We might call them coping mechanisms, or
maybe they are just habits that you have formed. Either way,
these things typically don't satisfy the way God can and wants
to. Based on the passage above, these "things" are typically
used in times of stress or anxiety.

Spend some time allowing the Holy Spirit to reveal the
"things" that you typically do or run to when you are feeling
anxiety or worry. Be honest with yourself. The first step to
healing is the revealing.

Finish these statements…

"The first thing I notice when I am anxious is…"

"The first person I talk to when I am anxious is…"

"The first thing I do when I am anxious is…"

"When I am stressed, I tend to..."

Now answer this question:
Who would I be if I ran to God FIRST every time I experience anxiety or stress?

> "You must catch the troubling foxes,
> those sly little foxes that hinder our relationship
> For they raid our budding vineyard of love
> to ruin what I've planted within you.
> Will you catch them and remove them for me?
> We will do it together."
> Song of Songs 2:15 The Passion translation

My One-Year Narrative

On a blank piece of paper, write a narrative that tells what your life will look like in one year. Be sure to include areas such as:

- Physically
- Emotionally
- Relationally
- Spiritually
- Education/Career
- Family
- Finances
- Physical environment

"In one year, my life looks like… "

After you have written your narrative, go back through each area and answer this question: What has to happen for you to get there?

"For this to happen, I would have had to… "

Finally, take time to really consider what barriers you will need to overcome to accomplish what you would need to do to get where you see yourself in one year. Consider emotional and mental barriers (limiting beliefs) as well as practical barriers.

"I would need to overcome… "

Purpose Discovering

Take some time to REALLY think about these questions and WRITE out some answers. You will get out of this what you put into it so don't cheat yourself... Grab a journal!

1. What excites you? (Makes you tick)
2. What upsets you? (Ticks you off)
3. What keeps you up at night?
4. When you were a child, what roles were you attracted to? How about as an adult?
5. What do you know already about what you were made to do?
6. What experiences have you had where you felt a strong sense of purpose?
7. What roles have you been in that you felt were an easy fit?
8. What would those around you say about what you are made to do?
9. What makes you forget to eat?
10. What are you willing to struggle for?

There are hints of our future in the celebrations of our past; places where we felt a sense of accomplishment. Spend some time recalling moments of celebrations in your life. Write these experiences down. Again, the more detail, the more revelation you will likely get. Be sure to include:

- What you were celebrating
- When you celebrated
- Why you were celebrating
- How you felt about it
- What it spurred in you

Take note of any common themes, but more than anything discover what excites you to the point of celebrating!

Your Strengths

Instead of focusing on strengthening our weaknesses, it has been found more beneficial to work on cultivating our natural God-given strengths. To do so, we must first identify our top strengths.

My top five personal strengths (think more about your character or personality):

1.
2.
3.
4.
5.

My top five professional strengths (think more about skills or abilities):

1.
2.
3.
4.
5.

How do your personal and professional strengths complement each other or how could they potentially work together to make you the "BEST" you in all areas of your life?

List ways where you currently see your strengths being utilized:

1.

2.

3.

List ways that you could intentionally be cultivating your strengths and utilizing them more:

1.

2.

3.

How do you think cultivating your strengths would bring more personal satisfaction to your life?

The Goal Connection

"You shall love the LORD your God with all your heart, with all your soul, and with all your strength." Deuteronomy 6:5

It is important that every goal we set is connected to the heart of God and what He wants for our lives. To ensure that each goal is both honoring to Him and excellent for you, take some time and go through this worksheet. This will help train you in setting good "God goals."

The Goal:
Write the goal in one statement.

The Spiritual Connection:
Take a moment to connect spiritually to this goal. (What would God say about it?) Write down why you conclude that this is a healthy "GOD GOAL" for your life.

The Head Connection:
Take a moment to connect intellectually with this goal. Write down why you conclude this is a healthy WISE goal for your life.

The Heart Connection:
Take a moment to connect emotionally with this goal. Write down why you conclude this is a healthy FULFILLING goal for your life.

The Strength Connection:
Take a moment to connect physically with this goal. Write down why you would conclude this is a healthy DOABLE goal for your life.

"You shall love the LORD your God with all your heart, with all your soul, and with all your strength." Deuteronomy 6:5

Using the mind's eye to envision what it will be like once you accomplish this goal is a great way to increase your odds of completing it. It is important that you connect with who you will be in spirit, soul, and body.

Visualize the accomplishment of this goal. In other words, rehearse in your mind what it looks like as already finished. Consider how you will feel spiritually, intellectually, emotionally, and physically. Record your thoughts.

Spiritually I envision myself:

Intellectually I envision myself:

Emotionally I envision myself:

Physically I envision myself:

Combine all that you wrote to complete this statement...

"Once I have accomplished this goal I will be..."

Read this statement every day until you have completed the goal!

What are your Tolerances?

One of the things that causes stress and anxiety is the feeling that we have no "control" in our lives. When we tolerate things that go against our design and the design for our days, we often find ourselves frustrated, exhausted, discouraged, and feeling overtaken or defeated. The first step to overcoming these tolerances is to simply identify them.

Take some time to consider what tolerances you allow in your life personally. List at least 5 of them below.

1. _____

2. _____

3. _____

4. _____

5. _____

Consider how your life would be different without those tolerances. How would you summarize the difference in one sentence? Write it below.

Is your summary sentence truer to who you really are and your design for life?

To squelch the lie that you "have no control" AND to begin to take back ownership of these areas, think about viable boundaries that you can set that will begin to remove these tolerances. Be sure to come up with at least one boundary for EACH one you listed above.

1. _____

2. _____

3. _____

4. _____

5. _____

Your Priorities

Consider this question...
Are your daily priorities lined up with your purpose?

Part of coming into the fullness of your design requires prioritizing that which is important to your purpose. Every decision you make today, every choice, every word, every action is either an asset or a liability to your future and your purpose.

Take time to consider how your daily priorities are moving you closer to your design or potentially slowing you down. Is there anything that needs to be removed? Is there anything that needs to be added? The goal here is to identify actions that will fill in the gap from where you are today to where you want to be, and then be intentional to prioritize them.

Things I need to remove:

1.

2.

3.

4.

5.

Things I need to add:

1.

2.

3.

4.

5.

Consider how your daily tolerances interfere with your design and purpose. (Refer to the tolerances worksheet).

Pick one thing from each list to start implementing for the next 30 days. Write below how you expect your commitment to affect you personally on a daily basis.

Your Wildest Dreams

Everybody has dreams and aspirations. This worksheet is all about giving you permission to communicate those dreams. If the sky was the limit (no barriers or limiting beliefs) what would you be doing or what aspirations would you be pursuing?

1. _____

2. _____

3. _____

4. _____

5. _____

Name some of the barriers that you currently face that keep you from pursuing those things you listed.

1. _____

2. _____

3. _____

4. _____

5. _____

Sometimes, we get so focused on the barriers that keep us from moving toward our dreams and aspirations that we don't "see" what CAN be done. Consider your options and take time to think about what you CAN be doing to fill the gap from where you are to where you want to be and what you want to accomplish.

1. _____

2. _____

3. _____

4. _____

5. _____

Pick 2 or 3 from the list above that you can resolve to start DOING and put a checkmark beside them.

Remember, action is how we move from point A to point B.

Find out if counseling/life coaching could be valuable to you!

Rate yourself out of a score of 10.

I feel purposeful _____/10
I am satisfied with my life _____/10
I am satisfied with my relationships _____/10
I am satisfied with my physical health _____/10
I feel a general sense of inner peace _____/10
I feel rested at the end of each day _____/10
I am generally excited about my day when I wake up _____/10
I accomplish most of my goals _____/10
My life feels organized and uncluttered _____/10
I feel like I am living life to my fullest potential _____/10

We are created to live life at 100%, anything less is settling.

How did you score out of 100 total? _____/ 100

*I am ready to take ACTION and enforce purpose into my life!
Yes / No / Maybe

To hire Lisa as your counselor/life coach, go to
www.lisa-schwarz.com

LISA SCHWARZ
Enforcing purpose

Lisa Schwarz is a national speaker, published author, Certified Biblical Counselor, Professional Life Coach, Brain Health Coach, and Founder/CEO of Crazy8 Ministries. She also designs and develops events, conferences, trainings and workshops for diverse settings throughout the United States.

Her mantra is enforcing purpose: maximizing who you are, what you do, and cultures around you.

Lisa has a powerful and effective mission that has broadened to include counseling, consulting, and coaching for individuals, groups, and organizations as well as a restorative housing program. All of this is to reach out and equip individuals, empower people, and enforce purpose in their lives through the transforming power of Jesus Christ.

Lisa has a passion for community and believes in the power of unity. For this purpose, she is driven to teach, train, and inspire others within her community and desires to be a catalyst for cultivating community collaborations; *together we are better.*

Lisa is involved in various community groups within her county including:

- Joshua Chamber of Commerce
- Cleburne Chamber of Commerce
- Burleson Chamber of Commerce
- Burleson Ministerial Alliance

She founded the Burleson Empowerment Project, serves as the Chairman for REACH Across Johnson County, is on the advisory board of Couch & Russell Financial Group, serves as a founding member of the Cleburne Chamber of Commerce Women's Leadership Initiative and as well as the Cleburne Charity Community Coordination. She is the secretary for the Burleson Character Council and is a part of the Community Health Needs Assessment Advisory Team for Texas Health Huguley Hospital. She also founded the Crazy8 Ministries' City on a Hill Festival held annually in Burleson, TX.

She and her husband, Brad, reside in Texas and have 6 wonderful children, a daughter-in-law, and a son-in-law.

Made in the USA
Middletown, DE
18 January 2022

59074298R00106